The Healing Epidemic

The Healing Epidemic

Peter Masters

THE WAKEMAN TRUST ✳ LONDON

© Peter Masters 1988
This edition first published 1988
Second printing November 1988
Third printing October 1992

THE WAKEMAN TRUST
Elephant & Castle
London SE1 6SD

ISBN 1 870855 00 0

Cover design by Andrew Sides

Printed in Great Britain by J W Arrowsmith, Bristol

Contents

Acknowledgements

I would like to express the deepest gratitude to all who have in various ways contributed to and influenced this book:

To the fellowship worshipping at the Metropolitan Tabernacle, who sponsored a Day of Special Studies on Divine Healing in November 1986, when the Tabernacle was crowded with pastors and Christian workers from throughout the UK. The ministry of that day eventually expanded into these pages.

To Professor Verna Wright of Leeds University Medical School, who gave two lectures at the Day of Special Studies and kindly consented to the reproduction of these as the final chapter of this book — *A Medical View of Miraculous Healing*.

To Professor John Whitcomb of Grace Theological Seminary, Indiana, USA, for his gracious and masterly Foreword.

To the staff of the Metropolitan Tabernacle, other friends and my wife; who processed the manuscript and proofs, contributing countless invaluable suggestions.

The God of all grace, who hath called us unto his eternal glory by Christ Jesus, after that ye have suffered a while, make you perfect, stablish, strengthen, settle you. To him be glory and dominion for ever and ever. Amen. (1 Peter 5.10-11).

PETER MASTERS

Foreword

DOES OUR GOD have sufficient power to heal all types of physical affliction today and even to raise and glorify those who have already died? Of course He does, for He said, *I am the Lord, the God of all flesh: is there any thing too hard for me? (Jeremiah 32.27.)* No true Christian will deny this.

Our wonderful God, however, has something more than mere *power*. He also has a *plan* and a *programme* for His world and for His people. Nothing is clearer in Scripture than the fact that God does *not* always do what He *can* do. For example, God *could* raise and glorify some dead believers today and a few more next week; but this would contradict *His revealed programme* for physical glorification: *Each in his own order: Christ the first fruits, after that those who are Christ's at His coming (1 Corinthians 15.23 NASB).* Therefore, it is neither His lack of power nor our lack of faith, but *His programme* which eliminates the possibility of occasional glorifications of believers.

When personal tragedy struck our family in the late 1960s, I became deeply concerned about God's ways with sick and dying believers. After nearly two years of serious illness, my wife died, leaving me with four children. There was much prayer on her behalf, and great confidence that God could raise her from the sick-bed. This He chose to do twice, in His mercy. But these healings were neither sign-miracles (like those our Lord and His apostles performed) nor were they permanent.

In subsequent years I searched the Scriptures and came to the following conclusions:

(1) God *can* do anything He *wants* to do.

(2) Even in Bible times, however, sign-miracles were very rare. Therefore it is obvious that God did not *want* to miraculously heal all true believers who needed such help.

(3) Toward the end of his spectacular ministry of miracles, even the apostle Paul could no longer heal people, because this was not God's will.

(4) God's plan for seriously sick Christians is not to go to faith-healers, but to *call for the elders* of their own local church to pray for them.

(5) Our Lord promised that the apostles would begin to do *greater works* than He did, namely, to preach the true Gospel of the cross and the resurrection.

(6) Some day, when Christ completes His redemptive purpose for His people through their bodily resurrection, our physical needs will be perfectly and permanently cared for.

Because of widespread confusion and misunderstanding in these vitally important questions, I commend this volume to God's people everywhere. Only His Truth can bring us freedom from fear and anxiety when pain and sickness come our way.

John C Whitcomb
Winona Lake, Indiana, USA

1
A New Scene

For the time will come when they will not endure sound doctrine; but after their own lusts shall they heap to themselves teachers, having itching ears; and they shall turn away their ears from the truth, and shall be turned unto fables. But watch thou in all things (2 Timothy 4.3-5).

TWENTY-FIVE YEARS AGO orthodox non-charismatic evangelicals could usually have cordial fellowship with old-fashioned Pentecostalists. In those days, when believers of such differing viewpoints were thrown together as students or during their time of military service, they found that they could often witness and pray together. Many of the old-fashioned Pentecostalists (seemingly rare nowadays) were conservative evangelicals, and whatever our differences on certain points we could respect them as fellow believers who were fully committed to the authority of Scripture as they understood it. But during the 1960s we saw the emergence of an entirely new brand of Pentecostalism — the charismatic renewal movement — and since then we have seen, as it were, a phase a minute!

With unbelievable rapidity charismatics have lurched from one excess to another, so that now we are confronted by a scene of utter confusion. Many in the charismatic fraternity have gone over to ideas and practices which come straight from pagan religions, and large numbers of young and impressionable believers have been spiritually corrupted in the process. Leading healers have arisen who unite the subtle tricks of the theatrical hypnotist with ancient occult techniques in their quest for results, and multitudes follow them.

Spiritual healing — carried out by gifted people — is being promoted in Christian circles as never before. Numerous 'best-selling' titles flood Christian book-stores to persuade the Christian public that it has a biblical pedigree, and healing seminars pack the largest conference halls in major cities across the world. We can no longer be interested in divine healing simply out of personal curiosity. The fact is that healing has become the chief attraction and propaganda tool of a new, crusading Pentecostalism which wants to perme-ate and engulf traditional Bible Christianity.

Divine healing has become the flagship of the charis-matic armada, the *pièce de résistance* at the charismatic banquet, and the main buttress of charismatic faith. Supposed incidents of healing are everywhere used to sanctify and justify a multitude of practices which cannot be verified from the Bible.

In many parts of the world the 'image' of biblical Christianity has been virtually ruined by charismatic extremists. In some countries, if one turns on a radio and scans the channels, one may hear any number of Christian stations broadcasting the programmes of charismatic healers who mingle outrageously unbiblical ideas with sentiments of real Christian Truth. The same is painfully true of religious television broadcasts in the USA.

This is surely one of the greatest triumphs of Satan, our malicious enemy, whose aim is to bring into ridicule

the Gospel of Christ. Satan is behind charismatic
extremists who claim to believe in the evangelical
doctrines of the Bible, but who at the same time mix
these precious truths with the poison of teachings which
are absolutely contrary to the Word of God. Nothing
could possibly delight the enemy of souls more than his
accomplishments in this area. How he loves to pollute
and ruin the godly and biblical image of evangelical
Christianity, so that we 'come across' as people lacking
in sound mind and rational judgement.

Yet despite the obvious peril many evangelicals —
particularly in Britain, Africa and the Far East — cling
on to the idea that they have a duty to smile upon all
points of view within the evangelical spectrum in order
to preserve evangelical oneness. If the Lord's churches
are infiltrated and ruined in the process, it scarcely
seems to matter. We have renounced our responsibility
to *warn* the flock of God, and have bared our throats to
the devil's knife. An inexplicable death-wish mentality
seems to have gripped the minds of Christian leaders.
Church after church has seen members — both adults
and young people — drawn into charismatic events,
bringing back the choruses, the ideas and the literature.

Christian periodicals have actually fanned the flames
of disaster by presenting the 'stars' of charismatic
extremism as reasonable and godly people who have
much to teach us! Leaders and periodicals alike have
failed to provide any serious analysis of the glaring
errors of the healing movement, thereby training God's
people to grossly underestimate the dangers involved.
Time and again the errors have been understated, with
the result that the churches remain unprotected and
unprepared for the militant tide of Pentecostalism now
sweeping across evangelicalism.

Before we survey the current healing scene in the
testing light of God's Word, we need to remind

ourselves of Satan's strategy for maiming the churches of Christ, for we have an enemy who is out to wreck and ruin our fellowships by any number of methods.

Authority of Scripture Undermined

First, Satan wants to *take away any serious respect for Scripture*. He wants to undermine and destroy its absolute authority over the lives of Christian people. There has been a spate of fine books in recent years defending the inerrancy of Scripture; but while evangelicals have been busy defending the *inerrancy* of Scripture, Satan has undermined the *authority* of Scripture. Right now there are countless charismatic innovators who are prepared to say, 'I believe the Bible is absolutely inerrant,' but they go on to say, 'yet the Bible is by no means the chief way in which God speaks to us, because He is also speaking to us through present-day prophets and prophetesses, and also through words of wisdom, words of knowledge, dreams, visions and sudden impressions. When we want to know God's will, or how we should do something, we attach great importance to these visions, dreams and other means of direct revelation from God.'

To these preachers the Bible has become virtually irrelevant. It has no authority at all. Sometimes they get round to checking some of their directly-communicated messages from God by the Scripture, but as the dreams, visions and words of knowledge are accorded permanent respect, this checking is usually a process of squeezing the Scripture to fit the ideas they already have.

What is the use of an *inerrant* Bible if we do not accept its *total authority*? What is the use of an inerrant Bible if it does not completely direct and control us? People do not really accept the authority of the Bible at all if they say, 'Yes, the Bible is absolutely inerrant but I do not believe it gives a detailed pattern for the church. I do not believe it must guide *all* our affairs. I do not believe that it addresses itself to *all* the things we must do. I believe that in many areas we are on our own under the direct guidance of the Holy Spirit.'

The devil's aim is to take away the authority of the Bible and he has succeeded supremely in the charismatic renewal movement, which regards supposed healings as God's stamp of approval upon all its activities.

Christians Rendered Gullible

On another front, the devil aims to *greatly increase the credulousness of Christian people* so that they become programmed to believe unbiblical nonsense and myths. This is what Paul tells us to expect when he says — *They shall turn away their ears from the truth, and shall be turned unto fables.* Satan wants ordinary Christian people to be vulnerable to exaggerations, stories, far-fetched things, lying wonders, and ultimately false doctrines and the lying representatives of Antichrist. He wants to get us to the point where we are merely superstitious people believing in magic and sorcery. Satan wants the 'spirit of a sound mind' to become extinct in the churches of Christ, and his instrument to bring this about is charismatic extremism.

When wonders and marvels wrought by the hands of man become a buttress to belief, then real faith is undermined. What a triumph for the devil if he can take away the faith of true Christian people so that instead of grounding their hope on what God has said, they come to depend on a constant flow of visible 'proofs', saying, 'I must see amazing signs and wonders! Let me meet people who can read thoughts, discern spirits, predict future events and effect stunning healings. Then I shall feel strong in faith!'

What a blow the devil strikes at the Lord when he succeeds in ousting faith from its high place, so that the attention of Christian people is diverted away from the Lord and His Word, and focussed upon so-called signs and wonders on earth! By this means the person and the Word of the eternal, ever-blessed God are snubbed and insulted.

True Worship Destroyed

Satan has yet another aim, and this is to *destroy all true worship*. True worship is that which comes from the *heart*, and which is full of *intelligent* appreciation and adoration of our glorious God. The devil wants to stop humble, reverent, rational praise rising from the creature to the Creator. To achieve this he has introduced into evangelical fellowships various forms of worship which are earthly, sensual and selfish. The object of this worship is that worshippers should enjoy themselves as they thrill to music, or work up exciting emotional sensations. Some people will throw themselves into orgies of ecstasy, while others will indulge their appetite for vainglory by appointing themselves as prophets, making awesome pronouncements to credulous gatherings. Significantly, the new approach to worship is chiefly promoted by the healing movement.

The new worship is 'all-for-me' worship. It is a thrill; a season of uninhibited release. It is a time when the rational part of a person may be subdued or discarded in favour of emotional escapism. This new worship is purely subjective, for it is all about *my* feelings, *my* moods, *my* health. It is not looking at God, leaning on Him, and worshipping *Him*. If the devil can pervert true, rational worship what a wonderful triumph he scores! If he can make people subjective and petty, how pleased he will be. If he can reduce a congregation of born-again people to superficial emotionalism, mystical mutterings, trembling and weeping, experiencing of physical sensations, clapping and dancing and banal, repetitive singing, then he will rob God of worship and render the church offensive to Him.

Genuine Conversion Obscured

Naturally, alongside all these aims, the devil wants to *wean churches from their zeal for true conversion*. Once again it is highly significant that leading teachers of the charismatic healing movement accept as completely valid the salvation-by-works teaching of the Roman Catholic Church. They tell evangelical people to accept the spiritual status of Catholic charismatic priests even though these have no sympathy with evangelical salvation doctrines. Protestant and Catholic charismatic healers share identical methods, recommend one another's books, and publicly endorse one another's spiritual standing. John Wimber, for example, must be assessed in the light of the fact that he regards Catholic healers — who reject evangelical doctrines — as 'converted' people filled with the Spirit. It is therefore obvious that his idea of conversion is not the same as Paul's, for the apostle pronounced the anathema upon all who taught another Gospel.

Without doubt the devil is seeking to erode away the old evangelical concept of conversion so that Christian people will eventually accept *any* religious profession or feeling as its equivalent. Then there will be no more real evangelism — only a vague call to people to join the church, any church, Catholic or Protestant — why should it matter? The charismatic healing movement has already done much to cloud the biblical definition of conversion, substituting a weak and shallow form of mere 'decisionism'.

Christ's Deity Denied

Supremely the devil wants to *detract from the uniqueness and the divinity of Christ*. What a mighty victory it would be for Satan if he could so injure our estimation of Christ that we sank to the level of the cults. Yet the most serious charge which must be laid against today's charismatic healers is that by their claims they literally deny the uniqueness and therefore the essential deity of Christ, as we shall demonstrate in the course of the following pages.

*   *   *   *   *

These are some of the devil's aims and objectives, but few seem to mind about the success he is having through the healing movement. Many traditional evangelicals still view this movement as though it were no different from the older Pentecostalism, but the longer this complacency continues, the more orthodox evangelical churches will continue to be infiltrated and lost.

For all the success of the charismatic 'revival', and its great multiplication of healing ministries, it has met with stern resistance from some evangelical groupings in the USA which have taken a clear stand against its teaching. Numerous American pastors have proved highly competent at warning their people about its errors. Nevertheless, even here charismatic healers steal tens of thousands of nominal Christians from traditional evangelical churches, a fact borne out by the spectacular growth of charismatic television shows.

In Britain, as we have noted, many evangelical churches have chosen to remain completely unguarded, and as a result charismatic infiltration has gone largely unchecked and unopposed, dividing and taking over an alarming number of previously sound causes.

It is imperative that we face up, even belatedly, to the frightening errors and dangers of the charismatic movement, and particularly its leading propaganda tool — the healing ministry. We must *prove all things*, testing the healing movement in the light of God's Word. We urgently need to equip ourselves to guide and counsel the increasing numbers of Christian believers who are troubled by the claims of the healers, and who are vulnerable to their plausible arguments. We cannot go on baring our throats to this influence, for we have an imperative scriptural duty to defend the churches of Christ, which He has purchased with His own blood.

We seem to have forgotten the case of the Judaising brethren in New Testament days. The Judaisers were people who got into the churches of Christ by making acceptable professions of faith. (This was the only way into New Testament churches, the rule for church membership in Bible times being — *with the mouth confession is made unto salvation*.) Perhaps many of them thought they really had experienced salvation. But very soon they began to express opinions which were completely contrary to their evangelical professions of faith, placing *alongside* the Gospel of grace, teachings which came from the corrupted Judaism of their former lives.

It seems that our generation of evangelicals has learned nothing from the troubles caused by the Judaisers. We behave as though infiltration and corruption can never happen, imagining that the devil will never use such methods in the twentieth century. Therefore, even when healers adopt pagan methods, as long as they claim to believe in the inerrancy of Scripture and in some form of conversion, we feel completely unable to repudiate them or their teaching. We even refuse to be on our guard. We obstinately refuse to learn from the New Testament that the devil's highest objective is to bring people in amongst us *privily* — ie: stealthily, secretly, as in *Galatians 2.4* — who will pass as Bible believers, yet who will teach destructive doctrines.

We have to face this today in the latest extremism of the charismatic movement, which now revels in direct revelations from God which destroy the time-honoured biblical foundations of worship and practice. Now is the time to sound the alarm and to save countless churches and believers from terrible disaster. We sorely need the salutary exhortation — Beware of the Judaisers!

2
Occult Healing Builds the World's Largest Church
The influence of Paul Yonggi Cho

THIS IS A PRAGMATIC AGE, and if something seems to work people are inclined to admire and respect it. Even people who should know better — evangelical people who are supposed to think with a Bible in their hand — have caught the spirit of the age. If some new method or phenomenon impresses them they will say, 'Well, this appears to be effective and great crowds are attracted by it. Why should we toil away with great difficulty in our traditional ways when by adopting this method we could probably get more success?'

In the course of reading a veritable pile of recent books on a range of charismatic practices including house groups, prophesying and healing, this writer has noticed that many of the advocates of these things have been powerfully impressed by the work of Paul Yonggi Cho, pastor of the largest church in the world, the Full Gospel Central Church in Seoul, Korea. They simply cannot keep quiet about him. Even as one reads the books the size of the congregation goes up; it is growing that fast! If a book was published at the beginning of the 1980s the author tells us that the largest church in the world has 150,000 members and over 100 assistant pastors. The latest books speak of 500,000 members. The church claims 17,000 new members a month, and many Western evangelicals are so overawed by this information that they just cannot wait to start experimenting with Yonggi Cho's methods.

American healer John Wimber is such a case. Before turning to charismatic healing he travelled round churches giving lectures on church growth. As he studied this subject he became increasingly depressed by the seeming ineffectiveness of Western evangelism by comparison with the phenomenal growth experienced by charismatic churches in Third World countries. He was particularly impressed by the claim that an estimated 70% of all church growth worldwide is achieved by charismatics. The extraordinary growth of Paul Yonggi Cho's church caught his attention, and he tells us so. Wimber realised that the growth of this church rested on its ministry of signs and wonders such as the casting out of demons and dramatic healings, and he concluded that Western Christians were experiencing blunted evangelism because they were afraid of living and ministering in such an atmosphere of spiritual power.

He tells us — 'Through the reports of signs and wonders from Third World students and missionaries, and through a greater understanding of how Western materialism undermines Christians' acceptance of the supernatural, I had begun to open my heart to the Holy Spirit. I wondered, were signs and wonders and church growth like those experienced in Third World countries possible in the United States? I would have to become a pastor again to find out.'

John Wimber's enthusiasm for Dr Paul Yonggi Cho's work is expressed in the course notes of his *Signs and Wonders and Church Growth* seminars: 'Full Gospel Central Church is growing fast because of an emphasis on healing. When Yonggi Cho prays for the sick in the Sunday service, many people are healed . . . After they are healed by God, they become Christians and good evangelists . . . this is the secret of church growth of FGCC.'

While Paul Yonggi Cho certainly cannot be regarded as the father of the new healing extreme, the extraordinary expansion of his church has caused numerous impressionable pastors and church leaders to fall at his feet as dead. Because of the influence his 'success' has had over so many, and also because his methods broadly typify those employed by other mega-churches in Latin America, it is obviously important to become familiar with these methods. Paul Cho's best-known book *The Fourth Dimension* reveals his theology, which marks a radical departure from historic Christianity.

Pastor Cho tells us how he learned to pray. When he began to pastor his church in Seoul he was very poor and living in one room. Then he wondered what he was doing trying to work without a bed, a desk and chair, or any means of transport, and he began to pray to God for these things to be supplied. He prayed very much for a desk, chair and bicycle, but after six months he was still lacking all three and became very discouraged. He tells us —

'Then I sat down and began to cry. Suddenly I felt a serenity, a feeling of tranquility came into my soul. Whenever I have that kind of feeling, a sense of the presence of God, He always speaks; so I waited. Then that still, small voice welled up in my soul, and the Spirit said, "My son, I heard your prayer a long time ago."

'Right away I blurted out, "Then, where are my desk, chair and bicycle?"

'The Spirit then said, "Yes, that is the trouble with you and with all My children. They beg Me, demanding every kind of request, but they ask in such vague terms that I can't answer. Don't you know that there are dozens of kinds of desks, chairs and bicycles? But you've simply asked Me for a desk, chair and bicycle. You never ordered a specific desk, chair and bicycle."

'That was the turning point in my life . . . '

Yonggi Cho tells us how he then began to specify the size of the desk (which was to be made of Philippine mahogany), and the kind of chair (one made with an iron frame, with rollers on the tips, so that when he sat on it he could push himself around 'like a big shot'). He thought long and hard about the kind of bicycle he wanted before settling for the ideal type and praying, 'Father, I want to have a bicycle made in the USA, with gears on the side . . . '

He then tells us how he prayed for his needs: 'I ordered these things in such articulate terms that God could not make a mistake in delivering them. Then I felt faith flowing up . . . that night I slept like a baby.'

Paul Cho says that the Lord never welcomes vague prayers. Taking the incident of the healing of blind Bartimaeus he seizes on the fact that Jesus asked this obviously blind man, 'What do you want Me to do for you?' as a proof that God insists on our making very specific requests. Until Bartimaeus was specific, Jesus did not heal him. At first glimpse, this idea of highly specific praying may not seem to be the greatest error in the world, but Paul Cho goes on to teach that the believer gets these specific requests supplied by visualising them and then bringing them into existence by faith!

It is vital to see this because here is the point at which charismatic development leaves Christianity and crosses into the territory of paganism. Ideas like this are the inspiration of the largest church in the world, imitated by so many Western charismatics. Note the following example given by Paul Yonggi Cho. While fulfilling a preaching engagement in another church he was asked by the pastor if he would pray for a spinster over thirty years of age who longed to get married but had so far not found a prospective husband. Pastor Cho asked her how long she had been praying for a husband, and she replied that it had been more than ten years. He then said, 'Why hasn't God answered your prayer for these more than ten years? What kind of husband have you been asking for?' She shrugged her shoulders and replied, 'Well, that is up to God. God knows all.'

Cho responded with these words: 'That is your mistake. God never works by Himself, but only through you. God is the eternal source, but He only works through your requests. Do you really want me to pray for you?' Calling her to sit down with paper and pencil he proceeded to ask a series of questions: 'If you write down the answers to my questions then I'll pray for you. Number one: now, you really want a husband, but what kind of husband do you want — Asian, Caucasian, or Black?'

'Caucasian.'

'Okay, write it down. Number two: do you want your husband to be as tall as six feet, or as small as five feet?'

'Oh, I want to have a tall husband.'

'Write that down. Number three: do you want your husband to be slim and nice looking, or just pleasantly plump?'

'I want to have him skinny.'

'Write down *skinny*. Number four: what kind of hobby do you want your husband to have?'

'Well, musical.'

'Okay, write down *musical*. Number five: what kind of job do you want your husband to have?'

'Schoolteacher.'

'Close your eyes. Can you see your husband now?'

'Yes, I can see him clearly.'

'Okay. Let's order him now. Until you see your husband clearly in your imagination you can't order, because God will never answer. You must see him clearly before you begin to pray.'

Pastor Cho then laid hands on the young woman and prayed, saying, 'O God, now she knows her husband. I see her husband. You know her husband. We order him in the name of Jesus Christ.' He then instructed her to paste the specifications for a husband on a mirror at home, read them night and morning and praise God for the inevitable answer. He teaches the need for a vivid mental picture coupled with a burning desire and a firm conviction that the goal is already accomplished.

Dr Cho calls this process: *visualising* the goal, then *incubating* it into reality by *strength of faith* — or would it be will-power? He teaches that believers may order up wealth and success; anything they want as long as it is moral. The key to getting these things is the art of fantasising them, because God cannot bring them into being unless the individual incubates the image. Certainly Dr Cho 'tidies up' his teaching by saying that people should first pray to God for what *He* wants them to have before fantasising and incubating these things into reality. But in most of his many examples (like that of the unmarried woman) he dispenses with the need to refer to God for guidance on the details. Though he attempts to give some biblical justification for his ideas, he tells us that he obtained them in the first place because God communicated them directly to him.

This is his own explanation of how he arrived at his teaching on incubating prayer answers and healing diseases. He tells us that he was driven to finding an explanation of how Buddhist monks in Korea managed to perform better miracles than those which his own Pentecostalist churches could perform. It worried him greatly that many Koreans got healing through yoga meditation, and through attending meetings of the Soka Gakkai, a Japanese Buddhist sect with twenty million members. According to Cho many deaf, dumb and blind people had recovered their faculties through these religious groups.

Cho was very jealous of the success which these other religions had in attracting followers. He wrote: 'While Christianity has been in Japan for more than a hundred years, with only half a percent of the population claiming to be Christians, Soka Gakkai has millions of followers ... Without seeing miracles people cannot be satisfied that God is powerful. It is you *[Christians]* who are responsible to supply miracles for these people.'

Other Korean Pentecostal pastors were also very troubled by these 'pagan' healings because ordinary church members constantly assailed them for an explanation. So, an anxious Paul Yonggi Cho fasted and prayed, looking to God for an explanation. It is noteworthy that in his account of his quest for a solution he makes no mention of looking in the Bible. 'Suddenly,' he tells us, 'a glorious revelation came to my heart ... explanations as clear as a sunny day.'* Dr Cho claims that God spoke to him describing the material world as belonging to the third dimension. In the beginning this three-dimensional world was chaotic, being without form and void, but the Spirit of the Lord (Who is said to dwell in the fourth dimension) brooded over it, visualising and incubating into existence a new order containing beauty, cleanliness, abundance and above all — life.

Then God told Dr Cho that because all human beings are *spiritual* beings (as well as physical beings) they have the fourth dimension in their hearts, and by developing

*The Fourth Dimension, p37.

the art of concentrating visions and dreams in their imaginations, they can influence and change the third dimension (material things) just as the Holy Spirit did when He brooded over the primeval earth. According to Cho, God told him that Buddhist and yoga adherents worked 'miracle' cures because they explored and developed their human fourth-dimensional power, *imagining* mental pictures of health and *willing* them into their bodies. God told him that all human beings had the power to exercise legitimate dominion over the material world through this fourth-dimensional activity.

Cho claims that the Holy Spirit said to him, 'Look at the Soka Gakkai. They belong to Satan . . . and with the evil fourth dimensions they carry out dominion over their bodies and circumstances.' Then God told him that Christians should link their fourth-dimensional spiritual power to God the Creator to have *even greater* control over circumstances than the Soka Gakkai. He concluded: 'Soka Gakkai has applied the law of the fourth dimension and has performed miracles; but in Christianity there is only talk about theology and faith!'

Dr Cho says that when Paul spoke of the 'inner man', he was actually referring to his fourth-dimensional power to visualise things and incubate them into life. (He does not explain why Paul fails to say one word about this himself, nor why Christendom has had to wait 2,000 years before this should be revealed through a personal revelation from God to Dr Cho.) Paul Yonggi Cho's teaching is a system of mind over matter (or rather, imagination over matter).

He frankly admits that it is a 'Christianised' version of precisely the same methods practised by Buddhists, exponents of yoga, and the followers of other pagan, mystical and occult systems. The only difference is that their fourth-dimensional power receives co-operation from the devil, while that of Christians supposedly receives help from the Holy Spirit. He says that so long as we keep our minds from foolish and wrong ideas, we shall keep the canvas of our imagination clean for the Holy Spirit to paint on it the things we are to have. In other words, direct guidance from God will come right into our minds. Once we receive this direct communication — which is literally God's will for what we may have and do — then we must *activate* it by the power of our fantasising and dreaming. Dr Cho sums it up saying — 'Your success or failure depends upon your fourth-dimensional thinking: visions and dreams. We see this principle in operation from the very beginning of Scripture.'

Abraham is claimed as an example of this process. 'How did a one-hundred-year-old man become the father of so many?' asks Paul Cho. 'He used fourth-dimensional thinking. He was full of visions and dreams. He learned to incubate in faith . . . By looking out in every direction, he filled his imagination in a concrete way with God's promise. He was not told to close his eyes when God spoke to him. He was to look at something concrete and substantive . . . So God expects us also to be active in the incubation of our faith by visualising the final results of His promise.'

Dr Cho makes the astonishing assertion that God showed this visualisation and incubation technique to Jacob in order that he could get enrichment from his uncle, Laban. When Jacob caused the vigorous sheep to pass between the 'speckled' rods of poplar, hazel and chestnut, he would stand staring at them, visualising spotted and speckled offspring. By visualising the desired objective Jacob activated the Holy Spirit Who — 'punched the proper keys for the necessary genes' (Dr Cho's words) so that Jacob's cattle began to give birth to spotted and speckled offspring.

Dr Cho says that his massive church grew to its

present size and continues to grow because he follows this principle of visualisation. He first imagines his church growing to a certain figure, and he then visualises all the faces and incubates the vision into reality. Similarly when he seeks the expansion of his television ministry, he imagines it being aired throughout Korea, Japan, the United States and Canada. He pins up maps of these countries in his office and he then develops a mental vision of the transmitters beaming the programmes.

He informs us that Sarah, like Abraham, had to visualise her child into existence. Yonggi Cho notes that at first she laughed at the idea that God would make her a mother at the age of ninety, but soon, he asserts, she got down to visualising the return of her youth. Where do we read in the Bible that she began to visualise the return of her youth? The answer is — nowhere, but as with every other assertion of extreme charismatic writers like Paul Yonggi Cho, the most amazing things are 'read into' the Scripture. Thoughts and actions are constantly attributed to biblical characters about which the sacred narrative says nothing.

Dr Cho has his own version of events when he tells us that as Sarah dwelt upon the promise of God a physical change soon began to take place in her body, with the result that King Abimelech found the old woman so attractive that he tried to take her as his concubine. Cho concludes — 'If a woman begins to think of herself as attractive, she can be. Not only will physical changes take place, but her self-image will change . . .'

Healing may be accomplished by precisely the same technique, and Pastor Cho tells the story of a man who was knocked down and terribly injured by a taxi while doing his Christmas shopping. When the pastor got to the hospital the man was unconscious and was not expected to survive the night. Believing that fourth-dimensional visualising was vital to his recovery Cho prayed that the man be given five minutes of consciousness.

Immediately the man recovered consciousness and Cho began to speak to him, saying, 'I know what you are thinking . . . you are already envisioning death. But God wants you to participate in the miracle that is going to take place. The reason you have regained your consciousness is that God wants to use your fourth-dimensional power and begin to paint a new picture upon the canvas of your heart. I want you to start painting a new picture of yourself in your imagination. You are on your way home and no accident has taken place. You knock on the door and your lovely wife answers. She looks very pretty. On Christmas day she opens up her present and you feel so proud you have such good taste.

'The next morning you wake up and have a good breakfast with your family. In other words, you are erasing death from your mind and you're painting a new picture of happiness . . . You leave the praying to me! I will pray in faith and you agree with me! Just use your ability to dream and see visions of your health and happiness!'

This was the way the man was taught to *incubate* the image of health. We have to learn, says Cho, to always visualise the final result and in that way we can incubate what we want God to do for us. He claims that the moment the injured man stopped *asking* God to let him live, and began to be *sure* that God was going to heal him, the bed began to shake and God performed a miracle.

Paul Yonggi Cho teaches that all Christians should aim to prosper in body, soul and spirit, and their success and failure in this is due entirely to their success or failure in visualising. He writes that his church members have so proved these principles of success that there have been no bankruptcies in his church, and the membership has undertaken the largest and most expensive church-building programme in all history. However, one cannot always take Pastor Cho's claims very seriously, for elsewhere he writes of how his own bankruptcy was all but inevitable, and how he stood on the very verge of suicide through the near failure of his church-building project. In the end he was only saved by church members taking such sympathetic action that many sold their homes and most precious possessions to bale him out.

Needless to say, when we come to the Bible we cannot find any of these instructions or ideas. We look in vain for any advice about visualising, incubating, imagining, or any other technique of sorcery or will-power designed to dominate God and to take away His sovereignty over the lives of His people. In the Bible we find that even an apostle like Paul is obliged to *ask* God in a humble, dependent way if he might be enabled to visit the people of a certain church — subject to the will of God.

The apostle Paul, judged in the light of Paul Cho's books, was a dismal failure because he knew what it felt like to be abased, to endure hardship and to encounter many, many difficulties. So often events did not turn out according to his wish or endeavour as a servant of Christ. Paul evidently made the mistake of negative thinking — *accepting* trials and tribulations. Overall he failed miserably in the use of his fourth-dimensional powers, never proving successful at fantasising or willing anything into existence.

To get God's guidance or blessing, Dr Cho teaches that we must ask the Lord to reveal His will by putting a desire for the intended thing into our heart. Then God must be asked to give a sign to confirm that the 'desire' is from Him. (This sign might amount to anything! A small coincidence will do.) Then, if we have peace about the desired thing we should 'jump up and go . . . miracle after miracle will follow you . . . constantly train yourself to think in terms of miracles.' Absolute confidence in ideas which spring into the mind as 'desires' is a characteristic of Dr Cho. Faith, according to his teaching, is not merely trusting that God will do those things which He has promised to do *in His Word*. Faith is redefined as having absolute trust in desires which come subjectively into one's mind, for these ideas or desires are assumed to be direct communications from God, and we must therefore develop unshakeable confidence in them. If we take these ideas and *imagine* and *incubate* them into reality, then we are promised 'miracles', and these should be our lifelong experience.

Paul Yonggi Cho soon added another stage to the process of visualising and incubating miracles — 'the creative power of the spoken word.' He says that he would often see on his 'mind's screen' a kind of television picture of growths disappearing, cripples throwing away their crutches, and so on. Then, he claims, God said to him: 'You can feel the presence of the Holy Spirit in your church . . . but nothing will happen — no soul will be saved, no broken home rejoined, until you speak the word. Don't just beg and beg for what you need. Give the word . . .'

Cho replied, 'Lord, I'm sorry. I'll speak forth.' Ever since that time whenever he has seen in his mind cripples healed or tumours disappearing, he has spoken out, saying, 'Someone here is being healed of such and such,' and he has named the disease. He claims that hundreds of people are healed every Sunday when he closes his eyes and calls out all the healings which he sees in his mind. Interestingly, the vision or revelation which he claims led him to this technique is strikingly similar to that which is claimed (some years later) by John Wimber, an acknowledged admirer of Cho's ministry. Like all 'healers' Dr Cho is forced to acknowledge that not everyone is successfully healed by his word. He cannot claim the infallibility of the Lord Jesus Christ and His apostles. He admits to many bothersome failures, but he claims that these are always due to lack of faith on the part of the sufferer.

Dr Cho expresses his disappointment that many Western people are bypassing Christianity and looking in Oriental temples for miraculous powers which he and others are now making available in Christian churches! He says, 'Evangelical Christians are increasingly understanding how to use their imaginations by learning how to speak the language of the Holy Spirit — visions and dreams.'

With all this in view we have no problem in identifying the strands which make up Paul Cho's new 'synthesis' religion. The Korean people have an ancient religion called *Sinkyo*, which sees the world as a 'religious arena inhabited by spirits'. Tragedies, troubles and illnesses can be cured by the *Mudany*, a woman priest who can interact with the spirits. She is the local 'medical priest', combining the roles of a medium and prophetess. She receives clairvoyant insights, goes into trances, casts out devils and cures diseases.

Korea has also for centuries been heavily influenced by Buddhism, particularly the form already mentioned which places great stress on healing and divining. It is taught that people do not need to be in bondage to their circumstances; they can, by right attitudes, by concentration, and by uniting with the eternal realm, get above suffering and sickness. The religious disposition of the Koreans is both harnessed and exploited by the 'Christianity' of Paul Yonggi Cho in his blatant mix of sorcery, mind-over-matter, self-interest, Sinkyo,

Japanese Buddhism and Christianity. But to mix pagan ideas and practices with the pure religion of Christ is condemned in Scripture as the heinous sin of idolatry. It is a marriage of Christianity and the occult, and is forbidden by Paul's words — *What communion hath light with darkness?* And — *What agreement hath the temple of God with idols?*

What has built the largest church in the world? The answer is, an idolatrous mixture of biblical teaching and pagan mind-techniques. God is deprived of His sovereignty in the believer's affairs, and the authority of Scripture is replaced by the authority of supposedly direct messages from God and the produce of the imagination. *This* is the kind of church which has moved hordes of impressionable Christian teachers the world over to jump on to the healing-prophesying band-wagon. We need to take very great care in these days.

Look at the books which charismatics and neo-evangelicals are writing today. They are commending these things. Look at healing advocates like John Wimber. They are deeply impressed by these things. These are the teachings which have captured their minds! This is the brand of Third World Christianity they are so anxious to emulate. What are we to say to these things? Remember the Judaisers!

3
East Winds Blow West
John Wimber's campaign
for occult-style healing

THE CHARISMATIC HEALING revolution has now passed
the point where a fundamental law of Christianity is
openly challenged and flouted — the principle that the
mind must be kept as a disciplined, rational faculty to
consciously direct all our affairs, and all our communion with God. By the exercise of this faculty we must
draw our knowledge of spiritual truth from the Word of
God alone. We may call this principle the Law of the
Sound Mind — *For God hath not given us the spirit of
fear; but of power, and of love, and of a sound mind*
[literally, a safe mind] *(2 Timothy 1.7)*. A safe mind is
one which is always in control of our thoughts and
actions, at no time allowing us to fall into trances,
visions, or other lapses of rational control. With this
faculty operating we never fantasise or imagine God
speaking to us, but we *hold fast the form of sound words*
(the Bible) with safe, thinking minds.

It is this law that has kept true Christianity distinct
from all forms of pagan spiritism down the rolling centuries. For years those who have engaged in tongues-
speaking (a loss of vocal control) have voluntarily laid

aside part of their rational faculty while they did so, but more recent charismatic literature glories in the total sweeping away of the control of the rational mind, pleading for believers to expose themselves uninhibitedly to the unseen forces of the spiritual realm. Visualising, fantasising, visions, direct communications from God and interaction with demons are all now the aim and the delight of the great majority of charismatics worldwide, along with clairvoyance, extra-sensory perception, mind-power, trances and mass hypnosis — all the techniques of Eastern healing cults. The Reformation gave people back their minds, sweeping away superstition and establishing the centrality of rational thinking. But new charismatic methods are bringing back the confusion and bondage of primitive spiritism.

If we look up the word *occult* in any dictionary we will find it defined as — that which is unseen, beyond the range of ordinary knowledge; involving supernatural, mystical powers or gifts. If we look up *clairvoyance* we will find it defined as the ability to see (mentally) things or happenings which are out of sight to ordinary people. All this is forbidden territory to Christians, involving forbidden pagan techniques, yet this is the 'religion' of charismatics today. Take the crusade of American healer John Wimber. He campaigns for Christians to undergo a gigantic *perception change* or transformation of outlook, detaching themselves from historic Christianity, and falling in line with the religious ideas of the East. He complains that Western Christianity is dominated by a scientific outlook and wrongly welded to rational ways of thinking.

Wimber claims that this is a purely *cultural* matter, pointing out that in the East and in African countries it is taken for granted that human beings may interact with the spirit world, and be in touch with things beyond the rational. He insists that it is a peculiarly

Western, cultural set of inhibitions which has caused Christians to be dominated by the world of the senses. To have access to power, John Wimber follows Paul Yonggi Cho in exhorting charismatics to open themselves more fully to other 'wavelengths'. They must be open to dreams, visions and impulses as a way of plugging into and reading the spirit world, particularly messages from God. They must cut loose from the chains wound around them by Western, cultural, scientific, empirical, rational inhibitions so that their souls become free to migrate into the dimension or territory of *spiritual* sense. They must learn to enjoy sensing and feeling the environment of the supernatural.

This is of course *totally* different from our historic Christian faith, where our minds operate wholly in the realm of the rational. By God's grace we accept the revelation of the Scripture as true and authoritative, and we take it into our rational minds. We do not ourselves make contact with angels or demons, nor do we receive *authoritative* messages from God outside His Word. Our rational minds are never laid aside for they are our highest human faculty. With them and through them we love the Lord and embrace His Word, and we receive the fruit of our walk as the power of God is poured out upon our lives.

As believers we have all experienced 'promptings' of the Spirit, when the Spirit in His goodness and grace livens up our thinking or sharpens our understanding. We have all received the help of the Spirit making us more shrewd than we would otherwise have been in some difficult situation. We have all been helped to remember duties or responsibilities which we would otherwise have forgotten, and perhaps we have all at some time been 'made' sensitive to someone else's great need when left to ourselves we would have remained insensitive. Certainly all of us know these kindly 'promptings', even though we may not always recognise the helping hand of God at the time. But such promptings and influences are the Holy Spirit's unobtrusive *help* to us; they are not the communication of Truth, nor are they *authoritative* directions.

All Truth and authoritative directions come from the Word alone, and every original thought of our own is absolutely subject to the principles and doctrines which God has given in his Word. God never communicates doctrines or authoritative instructions to us directly, nor does He enable us to tap into information about other people's lives or circumstances in a clairvoyant manner. We need to be keenly aware of the fact that the new charismatic teachings are very different from those of the old Pentecostalists of two or three decades ago. The new charismatics are not talking about someone receiving an occasional 'word of wisdom' from God which must then be checked against the Scripture. Nor are they talking about an occasional modern prophet, mistaken as that would be. They are now insisting that every believer should operate on this new, prophetic, supernatural plane — and traditional evangelicals must wake up to the horrific significance of this.

Charismatic renewal-movement teachers are saying that just as primitive tribes are supposed to be 'sensitive to the spirits in nature', so Christians are to be sensitive to the spirit world. They use the very language of animism and we should be stunned and shocked into a full realisation of just how pagan and unbiblical their teaching has become. John Wimber states that — 'throughout the New Testament there is continuous interaction between natural and supernatural beings (angelic visitations, dreams, visions, prophecies, etc). These interactions were one of the means of God communicating His desires and directions to His people.' His view is that this continues to be the norm for Christian instruction and guidance.

Anyone who does not accept that God communicates with His people in these ways today is accused by teachers like Wimber of forcing a rationalistic Western outlook on to the Bible. The fact is that traditional evangelicals believe that revelatory processes (with their attendant sign-gifts) were confined to Bible times because the Scripture itself says so. It is the Bible which limits revelation and authenticating miracles to Jesus and His apostles, calling these apostles the foundation stage of the Church.

It is the Bible which lists the very specific purposes for which the various gifts were given — purposes which were all accomplished during the first century after Christ. Later in these pages we shall list the Scriptures which prove, (1) the temporary nature of revelatory and sign gifts; and (2) the indispensable role of the rational mind. These are pivotal issues, both of which utterly disqualify present-day charismatic ideas and deny them any valid place in the life of a truly Christian church. We shall also review the main 'biblical' arguments which are offered by charismatic healers in support of their methods.

First, though, it is necessary to say that leading teachers of charismatic healing do not usually take up their ideas and methods because they discover them in the Bible, but as the result of other influences such as visions, dreams, and words which — according to them — God has spoken directly into their minds. Take the case of John Wimber, who can attract thousands of people to healing seminars held in many different cities around the world. How did this healer move from a fairly orthodox (though highly Arminian) evangelical theology to become a leading protagonist for the extreme charismatic front? The story of his background is provided in cassette tapes of his conferences and in two recently published books. (This writer found the books substantially less jarring than the cassette tapes in terms of grossly irreverent, even blasphemous remarks and jokes.)

John Wimber was a jazz musician converted through a house group in the 1960s. His conversion to Christ (described on a *Signs and Wonders* cassette tape) does not sound much like the experience of a person under conviction, whose heart opens to an awareness of personal sinfulness, and then to glorious Gospel light. He tells of how he became a Christian while bawling hysterically in response to his wife's conversion. According to his own account, his spiritual experience was born in total mental confusion and emotional frustration!

From the beginning he was a devotee of 'easy-believism', boasting that in his early Christian life he brought hundreds of people to Christ. As time went by he became pastor of an orthodox evangelical church, but eventually became disillusioned with his traditional style of ministry and took a seminary teaching post which involved visiting churches to speak on church growth. During the following three to four years he became 'especially impressed' by the effect which charismatic healing gifts had in accelerating church growth in many Third World countries, and began to take charismatic views more seriously. Acknowledging serious deficiencies in his own spiritual life over several years, he wrote:

'This influence came at a key time... I had been going through the motions of maintaining a relationship with God for several years — rarely praying and never reading Scripture devotionally. I was quite aware that I lacked a personal experience of God such as that described in Scripture...'

He was also feeling very disillusioned with the churches he visited, thinking that their efforts did not

much resemble biblical activities, and at the same time
he was going through a family crisis involving one of his
children. 'This personal crisis brought me to the end of
my tether emotionally and spiritually.' Eventually,
while travelling on a jet bound for Detroit, he experienced an emotional breakdown and began to cry help-
lessly. Feeling broken and humiliated he cried out in
prayer, 'O God, what's wrong with me?' He complained
to God that he was exhausted, suffering from high
blood pressure and constant headaches, and also that he
was tired of talking to people. 'For the first time in
nearly four years I opened the Bible to read it for
myself.'

However, it was not the Bible that turned him to a
charismatic position, but rather a sense of disillusion-
ment and dissatisfaction with his life and ministry.
Bearing in mind what he tells us about his considerably
backslidden state, there was clearly scope for him to
effect a fully satisfactory walk with the Lord within the
context of 'traditional' evangelicalism. If we fall, we
should not try to resolve our problem by abandoning
the Word and rushing off to some cult or 'ism for a fresh
start. However, in his despair John Wimber chose the
radical solution of charismatic experimentation.

A very significant influence upon John Wimber was
the fact that his wife had become an enthusiastic charismatic, leaving him rather out in the cold. Before he
came to share her opinions, his wife wondered if he
might possess the gift of healing. One night, while he
slept, she took his hand, placed it on her rheumatoid
shoulder, and prayed, 'OK, Lord, now do it!' A surge
of heat suddenly swept into her shoulder and John
Wimber woke up, his own hand hot and tingling. From
that day his wife was apparently healed.

The conclusive influence which turned Wimber to a
charismatic position was his conviction that God began

to speak to him in a direct and authoritative manner. He says: 'In the middle of the night I woke up: God was speaking to my heart. He said, "John, I've seen *your* ministry, and now I'm going to show you *mine*."'

One day a woman said she had a message from God to him, and when he agreed to hear it, she simply broke down and cried, sobbing for half an hour. Eventually John Wimber grew angry and said, 'Listen lady, your pastor said you had a word from God for me — what is it?' The woman replied — 'That's it!' In other words, God was weeping over John Wimber. The woman went on to say, 'God wants to know when you are going to use your *authority*.' Wimber stared incredulously at the woman and demanded — 'What do you mean?' But she could not elaborate on the meaning of the message, all she could say was, 'I don't know the meaning of them, I just give 'em!'

However, through God's direct communication with him, as well as through dreams, visions and other curious communications of the kind just described, Wimber came to the conclusion that God wanted him to use his authority to cast out demons and illnesses from people. He tells us that on nineteen occasions God spoke to him by 'dreams, visions, prophecies, tongues and Scripture' — Scripture being last in a very significant list. It never seems to have occurred to John Wimber that people who make dogmatic claims to have messages from God are setting themselves up in the place of God. They deify their imaginations and by so doing they become their own god. The inspired prophets and apostles of old were uniquely attested and authenticated by God, but what great and undeniable miracles had been done by the various 'prophets' who gave authoritative messages to John Wimber?

Similarly, he was not in the least worried about the 'messages' he received directly. At no time did he wonder whether his imagination might be over-excited. On one key issue after another it was not the Bible which provided the answer, but the voice of God in his mind. On one occasion John Wimber was puzzled about the healing of the paralytic man by the Lord Jesus, but he resolved his problems by simply asking God questions, and receiving direct and authoritative replies — thus dispensing with the need for study or commentaries! He sensed God giving him the following replies: 'Christians are called to heal the sick in the same way as they are called to evangelise . . . just as I give authority to preach the Gospel of forgiveness . . . I give authority to heal the sick.'

Wimber says that God commanded him to begin listening for His voice. Soon, he tells us — 'I began to hear His voice throughout the day.' Once John Wimber was facing and moving in this direction, almost every sermon he preached was on divine healing, and within a short time, he tells us, 'God spoke to me about having altar calls to pray for the sick after every sermon.' For weeks no one was healed and he became very despondent, determining to drop the whole matter of healing. 'Then God spoke to me clearly. He said, "Either preach my Word or get out."' He began to study the *way* Jesus spoke when He healed. He also read books like *Healing* by Francis MacNutt. (Father MacNutt is a Catholic priest, not an evangelical Christian. His books are given out at John Wimber's conferences.)

After four months of failure he was so distraught that at one meeting he threw himself on the floor and screamed his protests to God, saying, 'You tell us to teach what your book says, but you don't back up our act. Here we are; we're doing the best we can do — and nothing happens . . . it's not fair!' However at this time he was called to visit a church member confined to bed with a high fever. To his astonishment, when he 'mumbled a faithless prayer' this person was instantly healed. He left the house in great excitement, became euphoric and yelled to God, 'We got one!'

He tells us that on his way home — 'I was jolted out of my jubilant mood by an incredible vision.' In this vision he saw a great cloud, which turned out to be a honeycomb dropping honey from the skies. Below were people hurriedly gathering up the droppings. Then God spoke saying, 'It's my mercy, John . . . there's plenty for everyone. Don't ever beg me for healing again. The problem isn't at my end, John. It's down there.' This vision taught him to have faith to expect and secure healing for people instead of merely asking and hoping for it.

Influential healers like Paul Yonggi Cho and John Wimber, like other charismatic leaders, arrived at their ideas by influences *other than Scripture*. Only later did they turn to Scripture to find support for their ideas – a technique which is nearly always disastrous, for we know how easy it is to read any preconceived viewpoint into the Bible.

John Wimber now pursues a world-wide ministry of healing through large convention meetings. He is usually accompanied by a substantial team of fellow workers, and together they receive 'words of knowledge' in which they 'see' the illnesses of various people present in the audience, before praying for their healing.* Wimber's style is markedly irreverent, though this is now an increasingly common feature with the new wave of charismatic healers. He 'calls down' the Holy Spirit and orders Him around with language which is destitute of reverence, respect, awe and wonder. Many

*See the description of a Wimber healing campaign included in chapter 11 — *A Medical View of Miraculous Healing* by Prof Verna Wright.

candidates for healing are put into a state of hypnotic trance, supposedly by the Spirit's power.

One of the most serious (and blasphemous) aspects of teachers like Wimber is that they are ready and willing to diminish the Lord Jesus Christ in their desperation to find some shred of biblical support for what they do. In his healing seminars Wimber repeatedly denies the true and essential deity of Christ when he claims the ministry of Christ as a pattern for his own work. In the most explicit way he denies our Lord's divine character, detracting from His power and glory and reducing Him virtually to the level of an ordinary person. According to Wimber, Christ did not possess the personal power to read thoughts or to know the outcome of events.

The reason why John Wimber (like many other charismatic healers) has abandoned the Christ of the historic confessions of faith, is that he wants to make Christ our example not only for healing, but also for receiving 'words of knowledge' — direct impressions and commands from God. Obviously the Christ of traditional Christianity cannot be held up as an example in this respect, because He knew all things all the time. When Christ wept over Jerusalem, He knew exactly what would happen to that city in the year AD 70. When He set out to go to a town, He knew precisely what would happen when He arrived. He knew who would be healed, and who would believe on Him. Because of His divine character, Christ never needed 'words of knowledge', and so He cannot be heralded as our pattern or example for such things.

However, Wimber empties the Lord Jesus Christ of His divine attributes — particularly His foreknowledge — making Him totally dependent upon the Father for both information and orders concerning His activities moment by moment. He tells us that for a long time he could not understand why Jesus did not heal everybody who waited at Bethesda's pool, but, he claims, God suddenly gave him the key to understanding certain words of Christ. He says, 'As I was reading through the Gospel of John one day, the Lord spoke to me through the text which says, "I only do what I see the Father doing." If Jesus only did what He saw the Father doing, that means He never took the initiative. He was always operating under the unction, leading and guidance of the Father. He *only* did the Father's bidding . . . He was *always* under the Father's control . . . Whatever He did, He did specifically as the Father gave Him directions and leading.'*

John Wimber repeatedly emphasises this 'limited' divinity of Jesus as he strives to make Him a person whom we can legitimately imitate in *every* respect, including the receiving of intuitions from God, and the performing of healing works. If Jesus can be reduced to the stature of a mere man, then surely we can fully utilise *His* spiritual methods and thus do the same things.

Wimber has much to say about the account of Jesus meeting Zacchaeus in *Luke 19*, especially about His looking up into the branches of the sycamore tree and addressing Zacchaeus by name.** He asks, 'How did He know the name of Zacchaeus? Most of us would say — "Well, that's Jesus! He's the Son of God." But I want you to notice that the same guy that knew Zacchaeus' name didn't know how long the kid who was demonised had been in that condition. That same One that knew some things did not know everything all the time. Jesus operated both in His divinity and humanity

*Quotations are from the 'official' cassette tapes of a *Signs and Wonders* healing conference. Cassette 1984/8167, no.5, issued by *Vineyard Fellowship International, California, USA*.

**Signs and Wonders* cassette 1984/8164, no.2, issued by *Vineyard Fellowship International*.

and from time to time His information was limited, because Jesus operated in the Spirit, of the Spirit and by the gifts of the Spirit. I believe what we see here *[in the naming of Zacchaeus]* is a gift of the Spirit. Jesus looked up and said, "H'm, who's that guy?" And the Father said, "That's Zacchaeus. Tell him to come down!"' According to John Wimber, Jesus was obliged to operate by the Spirit just as we are, and He gives us the perfect example of receiving divine intuitions and 'words of knowledge'. Jesus could know nothing and do nothing without the enlightening and prompting given to Him by the Father, through the Spirit.

Today, Wimber claims, we should live and walk in this *identical* relationship with God. As we go, for example, into a restaurant or an airliner, we should be open to receive insights about total strangers. If we walk as Jesus walked, we shall suddenly be aware of the sins of one person, or the illnesses of another, and God will tell us to witness to one, and heal another. John Wimber's messages and books are crowded with anecdotes claiming such experiences. Be like Christ — he urges! Harness His spiritual secret, namely, words of knowledge and insights from the Holy Spirit, and you will duplicate His works. Make Christ your model in these things. Anything He could do, we may do also. After all, Christ was so limited by His human nature that He was not much different from us. Therefore if He, with the help of the Spirit, healed at a word, why should we not do the same?

Having detracted from the uniquely divine power and glory of Christ, John Wimber drags the Lord's mighty works down to the level of his own high-failure-rate psychological cures. He obviously does not think that Christ accomplished anything better than the puny 'works' which present-day healers claim.

Wimber even justifies his failures in healing by

asserting that Jesus had the same problem! He makes a blasphemous assessment of Christ's restoring of sight to a blind man *(Mark 8.22-25)*. Wimber says that the Lord effected this healing in two stages because He failed at the first attempt.*

All this is, of course, a blatant denial of the uniqueness of the incarnate Son of God. John Wimber, by many glib and irreverent remarks along these lines, fails the very first test of Christian orthodoxy and places himself firmly outside mainstream Christianity and among the cults, which all in one way or another detract from the divinity of our Lord and Saviour Jesus Christ.

It is a basic tenet of biblical Christian faith that Christ's divine nature was joined to His human nature in such a way that neither the human nor the divine was altered, diminished, or compromised in any way. Scripture is clear that Christ was — *the image of the invisible God . . . For it pleased the Father that in him should all fulness dwell . . . In whom are hid all the treasures of wisdom and knowledge . . . For in him dwelleth all the fulness of the Godhead bodily (Colossians 1.15 and 19; 2.3 and 9)*. In the light of such forceful texts how can anyone hold and teach that Christ's own knowledge was restricted so that He was dependent on other members of the Godhead for light and direction?

Countless charismatic teachers — and Wimber in particular — have become enemies of the most precious doctrine of our faith, that the incarnate Son of God, our Saviour, was (and is) — *the brightness of his [the Father's] glory, and the express image of his person . . . upholding all things by the word of his power (Hebrews 1.3)*. They deny (in effect) that — *the Word was made flesh, and dwelt among us (John 1.14)*. They refuse to

Signs and Wonders cassette 1984/8167, no.5, issued by *Vineyard Fellowship International*.

believe that Christ was the embodiment of all the knowledge and wisdom of God, needing no promptings or insights from outside Himself. They reject Christ's glorious, divine attributes.

When Christ said that He did nothing by Himself, but only those things which His Father taught Him (*John 8.28*), He *underlined* the fact that He was God, and that He acted as a member of the eternal Godhead. He also drew attention to the eternal harmony and oneness which exists between Father and Son. He did not say that he *lacked* knowledge, for He was the very Word of God made flesh! He knew everything, and by His own inherent power could read the thoughts of those around Him all the time. The disciples realised this when they exclaimed — *Now are we sure that thou knowest all things, and needest not that any man should ask thee (John 16.30)*. They had discovered that He knew their questions even before they asked them. *John 6.64* affirmed that *Jesus knew from the beginning who they were that believed not, and who should betray him*. Peter spoke of the power of Christ and declared that he and the other apostles were — *eyewitnesses of his majesty (2 Peter 1.16)* — literally His *magnificence, great might*, or *mighty power*.

We ask — How many young Christians have already been infected by the irreverence and blasphemy of the Wimber theology, with its heretical, low views of Christ? How many true believers have already forfeited their concept of Christ's power, honour and majesty? Only one Person in the history of the world could have the following lines written about Him, and that Person is Christ:

> *He could make the leper whole;*
> *Thousands at a meal He fed;*
> *Winds and waves He could control;*
> *By a word He raised the dead.*

How perfectly this basic and all-important doctrine of Christ's deity is described by the great hymnwriter Josiah Conder:

> Thou art the everlasting Word,
>   The Father's only Son;
> God manifestly seen and heard,
>   And Heaven's beloved One:
>
> In Thee most perfectly expressed
>   The Father's glories shine;
> Of the full Deity possessed,
>   Eternally divine:
>
> True image of the Infinite,
>   Whose essence is concealed;
> Brightness of uncreated light;
>   The heart of God revealed.

As ransomed people we are called to be faithful to the preciousness of Christ's divinity even unto death. We are therefore compelled to warn the churches of God to turn away from teachers who brazenly attack the uniqueness of our incomparable Saviour. We contend that the teaching of John Wimber is anti-Christian in its abuse of Christ, despising and discarding His divinity and glory in order to present Him as a 'humanised' example of healing techniques which may be copied in our day.

4
The Texts Say No!
Answering the pro-healing arguments

MANY OF THE ARGUMENTS advanced by the new charismatics in favour of their healing methods could easily sound convincing to young or unwary Christians because they *seem* to be scriptural. The reality is that not one of the texts which they cite supports their methods of healing, because Bible passages are constantly wrested away from their plain sense and obvious context. We must therefore be ready to expose the superficiality of charismatic reasoning if we are to save fellow believers from untold hurt and confusion. The arguments in favour of healing reviewed in the following paragraphs are used by a large group of charismatic authors, including recent writers such as John Wimber. To clarify matters, we define a charismatic author as one who advocates a healing ministry which includes most of the following elements:

(1) Healers will usually claim to possess a personal healing gift, and will probably practise the laying on of hands or utter words of command to heal the illness.

(2) It is believed that (as a general rule) all Christians

have a right to expect healing, as it is God's will and purpose that His people should be well.

(3) Clairvoyant powers are involved, either because the healer receives a 'word' from God about the illness without having previously met the sufferer, or because the healer receives a 'word' from God about the prognosis so that prayer can be made in line with God's will.

(4) Interaction with demons and exorcism are practised.

(5) Sick people are 'visualised' in a recovered state in order to effect the prayer of faith.

(6) The Holy Spirit is dispensed or called down upon sufferers.

(7) Trances or ecstatic states are induced to aid healing.

(8) The 'prayer of faith' is regarded as a prayer which is based upon an absolute certainty that God will heal.

By contrast, the traditional evangelical view is that all *direct* divine healing today is carried out by the Lord simply in answer to the prayers of His people. He no longer uses specially gifted people, but deals directly with the sufferer. Nor is there any promise of certain healing, for the Lord will act entirely in accordance with His sovereign, wise and perfect will, and sometimes it is His will to leave a burden of sickness upon His people. The proof of this and the Lord's purposes in allowing sickness are covered in the chapter, *Implementing James 5*.

The traditional view of divine healing also differs radically from the charismatic view in condemning the following practices as being disobedient to God's Word and highly dangerous: claims to the possession of clairvoyant knowledge; interaction with demons in any form; trances and ecstasies; healing by fantasising or visualising of results.

Here then are the arguments which are advanced by charismatic healers in support of their methods, with our replies. First among them is a general argument which is very obviously unbiblical, yet it throws off balance thousands of young Christians. After that, we comment upon the biblical passages which are used to justify charismatic healing methods.

1. 'Sickness is Satan's work!'

Many charismatic people hold that everything which is good is the work of God, while everything which is bad is caused by the powers of darkness. As it seems inconceivable to them that God could be responsible for sickness, they conclude that all sickness is from the devil and his demons. By this reasoning they arrive at the view that sickness is *never* God's will for His people. With almost unbelievable ignorance of elementary Christian theology, healer Colin Urquhart writes, 'Jesus clearly saw sickness as Satan's work.'

Such writers are out of touch with the most basic doctrines of the Christian faith because the Bible teaches that when mankind fell from obedience to God, a curse or punishment was placed upon the world *by God* which removed the full and glorious blessing of God and brought the principle of death into the world. Ever since that time nature — including the human body — has been entirely different. Everything is now subject to change and decay. Death and the forces of wear and erosion operate in our universe in accordance with the sentence pronounced upon mankind — *Dust thou art, and unto dust shalt thou return*. The special favour of God's co-ordinating hand no longer guarantees perfection and order in life, or the uninhibited growth of crops and fruits, for a tendency to chaos and disorder has invaded all nature so that men must sweat to clear the thorns and thistles of the field for their food and survival.

The sorrow of conception, the cursed ground and the necessity of daily work all stem from the fall of man and his punishment in the garden of Eden. All who are in this world, believers and unbelievers alike, share the same fallen world, the same altered biology, the same fallible bodily components, the same hostile, germ-laden environment, the same vulnerable, decaying, dying bodies. All these things are part of God's righteous judgement upon the human race. Furthermore they are strokes of God's rod of mercy, because by these things God teaches the human race about its lost estate, humbling, chastising and warning all people that they are sinners in the hands of an offended God.

Satan has not placed the curse upon this world. He did not introduce the biology of death. It was God Who withdrew the special blessings which made Eden a paradise on earth, and changed all nature by a single pronouncement (*Genesis 3.14-24*). Satan should not be credited with the judicial acts of the sovereign God! Far from being responsible for the curse, Satan is himself a victim of it, having been sentenced to be a squatter and a fugitive spirit by God, until his head be crushed at the coming of the woman's promised seed — the Lord Jesus Christ.

The simplistic notion that demons must be behind all illness stems from a failure to realise that God Himself has sealed the world under its present circumstances in which the principle of death and decay pervades all nature. Satan can only cause illness when he takes over the personality of someone who has invited him to do so in ways which we list in the chapter, *Demons, Demons Everywhere!* However, though Satan cannot cause illnesses, in the case of sick believers he can and does take advantage of these illnesses by directing at them salvos of temptations, as well as gloomy, discouraging thoughts.

When Paul suffered a thorn in his flesh it was *given* to him by God to save him from becoming puffed up as the result of receiving glorious revelations. It was not planned or given by Satan, though Paul tells us that it became the means (the angel or *messenger*) by which Satan communicated despairing and discouraging thoughts and temptations to him. Nevertheless, Paul does not say that Satan *caused* his disability, only that he took advantage of it. The thorn was designed and given by the Lord, Who also designed the comfort and grace which was put alongside it as Paul prayed.* To view sickness as Satan's work is to exchange the clear teaching of the Bible for the primitive ideas of pagan dualism. Yet this is the most popular way of explaining sickness in current charismatic books, showing how far the healing writers drift from our biblical heritage.

2. 'God promises health'

A popular justification of healing ministries is the health promise repeatedly made in the wilderness to the ancient Israelites, eg: *I will put none of these diseases upon thee . . . for I am the Lord that healeth thee (Exodus 15.26)*. It is confidently assumed that if God's will was to heal His people in those days, then it must be His will that Christians should be healed today. But of course, this does not follow at all! All the healing promises recorded in the early books of the Bible were made very specifically to the nation of Israel as a *nation*, and were conditional upon their keeping all His commandments (moral and ceremonial) and driving the Canaanites out

*The proof that Paul's thorn was a physical affliction is given in an appendix to the chapter, *Implementing James 5*.

of the promised land. There were other promises also which applied only to that nation and only for that particular time.

Take the promises that the Israelites would be led to a special country of their own *on earth*, and (if obedient) would be protected from all earthly enemies. It does not follow that Christians today will be given an exclusive geographical land and shielded from all persecution and oppression. Israel was also promised great prosperity in return for obedience, but we know that New Testament believers are frequently called to endure great hardship for the Lord.

We must always remember that God had a special purpose for the Israelites. During the period of that old covenant God was teaching them (and teaching the world through their experience) numerous fundamental lessons, such as the principle that sin must be punished and obedience to God will be blessed. If we give our children sweets when they are good, it does not follow that we intend to keep them supplied with sweets all their lives. Likewise, God's arrangement to heal, defend, and settle in a special land the Israelites of old was all part of His teaching programme for the 'church' in its infancy. The principles which continue are that God will heal our spiritual wounds, defend us from our spiritual enemy (Satan) and lead us to our spiritual home (Heaven).

We should not be surprised that God did some rather special things for the ancient Israelites, because He put them through some rather hard experiences in order to fulfil His purposes. He called them, for instance, to endure a hard wilderness environment, to conquer an evil land, and to pioneer new homesteads. In His kindness, and to prove Himself to them, He gave them many unique blessings such as the provision of miraculous bread for which they exerted no labour, and other miraculous provisions also. They were promised that none of them would suffer infertility, miscarriages or premature deaths. These promises were made to the nation *as a whole* although they did not enjoy the benefits of them for long because of their disloyalty to the terms of God's covenant.

What happened to godly individuals when the time came that the *nation* as a whole forfeited the promised physical benefits? Did believing individuals get these blessings? The answer is that they did not. When the nation as a whole suffered famine, enemy attack, poverty, and the inability to drive out the Canaanites, then godly individuals generally had to suffer the same trials. In other words, the special physical blessings, including complete protection from all forms of illness, were designed for the nation as a whole, and could not be claimed as a right by individual people.

3. 'The Israelites were never sick'

To consolidate the idea that God desired His Old Testament people to be always healthy it is asserted that sickness only came upon people when they were sinful — the obvious example being Saul's insanity. John Wimber is so sure of this he states: 'Job is the one exception.' He then attempts to dismiss Job from the reckoning by saying, 'Most of his suffering was not sickness.' This is a hopeless attempt to side-step the issue, for the book of *Job* utterly demolishes the idea that only sinful people were sick, devoting much of its space to proving that the state of health or wealth of a person is no indication whatsoever of his standing with God.

In any case, Job is certainly not the only example of a righteous person who suffered illness. The dogmatic statement that righteous people were not sick in those days is typical of the countless amazing and groundless assertions made by charismatic authors like John Wimber. The danger is that young and impressionable believers may trust such statements. They may not know about Jacob's mortal sickness in *Genesis 48*. They may not know about Elisha's sickness and death, or Daniel's sickness, which was actually the result of receiving a revelation which overawed the prophet's human constitution.

What about David? Is it seriously being suggested that *all* his infirmities were the chastening hand of God (as some certainly were)? What about *Psalm 22*, a Messianic prophecy rooted in a painful affliction suffered by David as a type of Christ? Here David describes an intense struggle with death, including emaciation and exhaustion, possibly a condition of both mind and body brought about while he was weakened under the burden of intense persecution.

How can charismatic healers say so dogmatically that sickness in the Old Testament was *always* the result of personal sin? What about Abijah in *1 Kings*, the child who died because he was the only one who was *not* sinful? And what about the child healed by Elijah — was he being punished for sin?

The standard of biblical knowledge and interpretation exhibited in some of these pro-healing arguments is often very poor, but then, the presenters of these arguments usually attach much more importance to their own visions, dreams and direct messages from God than they do to the Bible. Our purpose is to appeal to believers who are impressed by such arguments not to be so trusting. As soon as they check the Scripture quotations for themselves they will discover just how weak the quality of argument is, and how inappropriate the verses cited.

4. 'Jesus is our example'

To anyone who has not yet learned the biblical reasons for our Saviour's healing ministry the case advanced by charismatic healers may seem especially powerful. It appears to be so simple and so logical: 'Jesus healed the sick, and He is our example and pattern.' Most healing writers reason that Jesus spent such a lot of time healing people physically that we must conclude that it is our duty to do the same.

One claims that — 'It is always God's best purpose to heal . . . Jesus did not have long prayer sessions with His Father enquiring whether He wanted to heal; He knew what His Father wanted to do' (Urquhart). Another writer says, 'Healing is what God wants done in the world and it is our responsibility to see it is carried out' (Glennon).

Most charismatic writers list a number of reasons *why* Jesus healed, but strange to say, they nearly all omit to mention the most important reason of all — the reason which sweeps away the whole basis of charismatic healing. Jesus did not heal in order to be an example to us, but in order to authenticate His divine nature and power; to demonstrate that He was the long-prophesied Saviour sent from God. In *John 20.30-31* we read — *And many other signs truly did Jesus in the presence of his disciples, which are not written in this book: but these are written, that ye might believe that Jesus is the Christ.*

John also records — *This beginning of miracles did Jesus in Cana of Galilee, and manifested forth his glory; and his disciples believed on him (John 2.11).* In *John 5.36*, the Lord Jesus says — *The works which the Father hath given me to finish, the same works that I do, bear witness of me, that the Father hath sent me.* The purpose of all the healing miracles was certainly to manifest the compassionate and merciful character of Christ, but pre-eminently it was to *authenticate* Him as the promised Messiah. In exhibiting His power and glory He healed not merely the functional disorders but also the most deep-seated, organic disorders. He restored sight, renewed crippled, wasted limbs, and raised the dead (never once failing) to establish His messiahship for all time — that was the reason given in the Scriptures for Christ's healing miracles.

Charismatic writers therefore miss the whole point of our Lord's great miracles in thinking that they should be able to do the same things, but their argument is defective on yet another count. If we are supposed to follow the example of Jesus in our healing, why can present-day healers not achieve the Lord's results? Why do they succeed only in 'healing' the *kind* of conditions that numerous hypnotherapists or non-Christian cult healers can also cure? And why do so many of the people who think they have been healed later change their minds? If the Lord's healings are supposed to be a pattern for us, then absolute success in all cases which present themselves, including the blind, withered and at times even the dead, must be the standard.

5. 'Jesus told His disciples to heal'

Most advocates of charismatic healing rush from the supposed example of the Lord to the commissioning of the twelve, and later the seventy disciples (eg: *Luke 9* and *10*). Did not these disciples receive a 'pattern' command with — *power and authority over all devils, and to cure diseases*? Were not the seventy told to *heal the sick* as they announced God's message? All the charismatic healers unite to say that the task given to these disciples was an ongoing task for all disciples in the subsequent history of the church, but they are wrong again, because the reason why Christ gave those disciples their power (which was temporary) is clearly stated in the Gospels. In fact, everything about these two missions was related to a unique, 'one-off' task.

We note that the assignment given to the twelve was that they must go *exclusively* to Jewish people, and not to Gentiles. They were to heal *every* illness, and also raise the dead. They were forbidden to accept any money and they were to take no bag, not even a change of clothing, for they were to rely entirely on hospitality for their survival. All this is recorded in *Matthew 10.5-10*. The seventy were sent on an equally specific mission, for they were to do no more than to visit the towns which the Lord Jesus would soon visit personally, and their mission was given the same conditions as that of the twelve. The purpose of their visitation was to heal the sick in Christ's name and say, *The kingdom of God is come nigh unto you,* thus heralding the visit of the Messiah to the Jews of that time.

Jesus was, in effect, saying to the covenant people, 'By these powerful signs, done in My name, you will know that the kingdom of God has come and a new age has dawned. Your promised Messiah has come!' In no way were these missions a pattern for the 'normal' work of disciples, as we can tell from the very limited duties which they were assigned. Would the Lord wish us to restrict *our* mission to Jews? Does He forbid His missionaries today to accept payment or to possess a change of clothing? Does He command us to be entirely dependent upon local hospitality? Why do charismatic healers not want to take *all* the elements of these missions as a pattern for their conduct?

The final proof that these were unique and temporary activities is given in *Luke 22.35-36* where the Lord refers to the special missions as something belonging to the past, setting new rules for the future work of the disciples. He is soon to be rejected by the nation of

Israel and so the days of bounteous healing (to mark His coming) will be over. Healings in the future will be less frequent and confined to the apostolic band. When the great commission is given in *Matthew 28.16-20* (other allusions to this commission are in *Luke 24.45-48* and *Acts 1.8*) there is no mention whatsoever that the dispensing of healing miracles will be an ongoing activity of the messengers of God. There is only one passage which makes any mention of healing, and this was addressed exclusively to the disciples who were the future apostles, as we shall now show.

6. 'Jesus promised signs following'

The exception to the commissioning passages just referred to is *Mark 16.14-18*, which includes the promise of the signs following: *And these signs shall follow them that believe; in my name shall they cast out devils; they shall speak with new tongues; they shall take up serpents; and if they drink any deadly thing, it shall not hurt them; they shall lay hands on the sick, and they shall recover.*

Why is this 'version' of the great commission different from the others, in that It includes healing, exorcism and protection from snake bites and poisons? The answer is that it was given to the disciples *privately* in a separate appearance from the later, more 'public' giving of the commission in Galilee. The *terms* of the commission are quite different in the *Matthew* and *Mark* accounts. The *Mark* occasion occurred while the disciples *sat at meat*, while the *Matthew* occasion occurred out in the open on a mountain previously designated by the Lord. Most commentators think that the latter was the same event which Paul refers to in *1 Corinthians 15.6*, when the risen Christ was seen by over 500 people. The *Mark* occasion was therefore first, took place at Jerusalem and was a private briefing for the eleven disciples, who would be the future apostles.

Mark 16.14 provides the context and the key to Christ's private commission to the eleven — *Afterward he appeared unto the eleven as they sat at meat, and upbraided them with their unbelief and hardness of heart, because they believed not them which had seen him after he was risen.* The Lord's chief purpose was to reproach the eleven for their *unbelief and hardness of heart.* This is the point of His statement to them, and this must be kept in mind as we read through the passage. As Jesus reproaches them, He gives them their commission in brief form — *Go ye into all the world, and preach the gospel to every creature. He that believeth and is baptized shall be saved; but he that believeth not shall be damned.* Hearers who believe will be saved, those who do not will be lost.

Having stated their task, the Lord returns to the problem of the disciples, all or some of whom have unbelieving and cold hearts. In remonstrating with *them*, He says: — *And these signs shall follow them that believe . . . (Mark 16.17).* He is not now talking about those who believe their preaching, but of the apostles themselves. If *they* will dedicate themselves to obey the commission, believing their Saviour, then — *In my name shall they cast out devils; they shall speak with new tongues; they shall take up serpents; and if they drink any deadly thing, it shall not hurt them; they shall lay hands on the sick, and they shall recover (Mark 16.17-18).*

This interpretation of the passage is correct because it holds on to the *subject* which Mark announces as the theme of these verses — which record *how* Jesus reproved the unbelief of the disciples. How did He do this? First, He reproached them. Secondly, He told them their duty. Thirdly, He promised them that authenticating signs would follow those apostles who believed and obeyed. The correctness of this interpretation is further confirmed by the known facts. Only the apostles (plus three immediate helpers or appointees) actually healed people according to the *Acts* record, and as far as snake bites are concerned, only Paul is recorded as having survived one. Tongues-speaking certainly extended beyond the apostolic band, but the other signs did not.

Mark 16.17-18 is really a very embarrassing text for charismatic healers, for while they claim that Christ has promised these signs for all time, they cannot survive snake bites and poisons. Until they can, they should realise that they are wresting this text out of its proper context, namely that of a private exhortation to the future apostles. The version of the great commission which applies to all disciples — of every day and age — gives us no instruction to perform healing signs.

7. 'Healing is in the atonement'

One of the arguments advanced by charismatic healers is that sickness, like sin, has been atoned for on Calvary and therefore healing should run alongside forgiveness in the ministry of the church. *Matthew 8.16-17* reads — *When the even was come, they brought unto him many that were possessed with devils: and he cast out the spirits with his word, and healed all that were sick: that it might be fulfilled which was spoken by Esaias the prophet, saying, Himself took our infirmities, and bare our sicknesses.*

Matthew refers to *Isaiah 53.4-5*, those well-known words — *Surely he hath borne our griefs, and carried our sorrows: yet we did esteem him stricken, smitten of God, and afflicted . . . and with his stripes we are healed*. The word translated *griefs* in this passage is indeed the Hebrew word for sickness, and Isaiah certainly says that we are *healed* by the wounds of Christ. Without doubt the

Saviour bore away for us on Calvary both the *punishment* for sin and the *consequences* of sin, which include all the results of the curse — disease, suffering, misery and death. On Calvary He bought the right to deliver us from our *spiritual* sicknesses and also our *physical* diseases, and therefore there is no doubt that bodily restoration is purchased in the atonement.

But it does not follow that this bodily restoration is wholly available *now*. Not all the blessings which were purchased for us in the atonement are available now. Most notably we may think of deliverance from death — *God so loved the world, that he gave his only begotten Son, that whosoever believeth in him should not perish, but have everlasting life.* This has reference to the *soul* and to the *future life*, for the present body will perish and die and its restoration is a future event. Jesus raised the dead, but it does not follow that we are to raise from the dead all Christians who die, for this benefit of the atonement lies in the future.

So it is with healing. If the Lord, in answer to prayer, grants that we recover from an illness, we remember that He purchased the right to forgive and heal us by bearing away the *consequences* of sin on Calvary. But the principal fruit of this aspect of our Lord's atonement lies in the future, when all sickness and bodily decay, including death, will be swept away for ever, and we go to be with Him in paradise. The healings which we may experience now are merely a token of that coming deliverance.

When the Lord Jesus Christ was on earth He healed sicknesses as a sign and a demonstration that He was the Messiah prophesied by Isaiah, and that He would take care of both the problem of sin, *and* the problem of its consequences — suffering, sickness and death. He exhibited His power over such ills, but He did not promise a general dispensation of healing for those who believed; He promised a dispensation of repentance and remission of sin. The ministry which is committed or entrusted to us as Christ's messengers is called by Paul — *the word of reconciliation.* Forgiveness is the great atonement benefit which we preach to all; healing is principally a benefit for the future, although kindly tokens are given now to believers who humbly pray for them. To elevate healing to a position alongside forgiveness of sins and to herald perfect health as a guaranteed benefit of the Cross available now, is to wrest the meaning of *Isaiah 53* so that it contradicts and conflicts with clear New Testament statements that our mortal bodies must wait for their full deliverance from malfunction and decay.

8. 'Conversion includes healing'

Several healing writers make much of Paul's 'new creature' text in support of their healing ideas — *If any man be in Christ, he is a new creature: old things are passed away; behold, all things are become new (2 Corinthians 5.17)* Paul's words are evidently supposed to prove that bodily health goes with the new birth as an immediately available benefit of coming to Christ, but these writers do not stop to ask what the apostle is talking about. When he refers to a *new creature* does he have in mind just the spirit, personality and character of the believer, or does he mean to include the body as well? If charismatic writers would only take the trouble to glance at the surrounding verses they would quickly discover the answer, for in the same chapter, Paul shows that conversion leaves us still dwelling in a bodily tent which retains many built-in disadvantages — *For we know that if our earthly house of this tabernacle were dissolved, we have a building of God, an house not made with hands, eternal in the heavens. For in this we groan, earnestly desiring to be clothed upon with our house which is from heaven (2 Corinthians 5.1-2).*

There are so many passages which tell us that our *bodies* have yet to receive their new-creation redemption. Bodily resurrection is yet to come, and only then shall we have bodies which are freed from all aches and pains, problems and trials. *Romans 8.18-25* is a marvellous passage which charismatic healers seem not to understand at all: *For I reckon that the sufferings of this present time are not worthy to be compared with the glory which shall be revealed in us. For the earnest expectation of the creature waiteth for the manifestation of the sons of God . . . Because the creature itself also shall be delivered from the bondage of corruption.*

Whether we are pastors, teachers or mature church members we must be active in showing these basic biblical principles to those who are young in the faith so that they will recognise the alarming superficiality of charismatic writers in their misuse of texts.

9. 'The early church had constant miracles'

Charismatic writers all convey the impression that healing miracles occurred constantly throughout the early church. Says one: 'The almost casual way in which the various instances of healing are recorded in the narrative shows that it was looked upon as an everyday occurrence' (Glennon). Says another, 'Clearly, healing was not limited to the apostles' (Urquhart). If we are suspicious of John Wimber's boasts and stories about signs and wonders he simply retorts that our cynicism 'demonstrates how far Christianity in Western society has drifted from experiences that were *everyday occurrences* in New Testament times' *[italics ours]*.

Is this true? Canon Glennon is very scathing about the traditional view which confines healing to the apostolic band, and says that it is a view 'for which there is not one word of justification in the Scripture'. But when the same author spreads out his texts to prove that *everyone* healed, the amazing thing is that he cannot find one single text in which an 'ordinary' Christian healed anyone of an illness! Neither can any of the other healing advocates. Every example of healing (by the instrumentality of a person) in the book of *Acts* is performed by an apostle, or an apostle's deputy,* and if we go *strictly by the biblical record*, the only three 'deputies' who had any involvement in healing were Stephen, Philip and possibly Barnabas if *Acts 14.3* includes him. (We shall comment in a moment on the hypothetical possibility that there were others also.) Outside this select group there are no 'gifted' healing activities actually recorded in *Acts* or the epistles. Indeed, by the time the letter to the *Hebrews* was written (AD 64-68) the writer was already looking back at the healing miracles performed by human agency as a thing of the past (*Hebrews 2.4*).

The idea that healing miracles were performed everywhere and all the time is a complete illusion, yet all charismatic authors claim that this was the atmosphere of the early church. They bombard their readers with texts and incidents, working up an impression of constant signs and wonders as they go, but they fail to point out that all the texts which they quote refer exclusively to the apostles and no more than three apostolic messengers or assistants. In these days of charismatic confusion we need constantly to draw attention to the texts which prove that signs and wonders were peculiar to the

---

*The singular case of Ananias laying hands on Saul (*Acts 9.17*) after receiving a vision from the Lord, is hardly a case of healing, as Saul had been temporarily blinded by the Lord, and Ananias was sent (as one of those whom Saul persecuted) to seal God's forgiveness and acceptance of him.

apostolic band, and were not bestowed generally. *Acts 2.43* reads — *Many wonders and signs were done by the apostles. Acts 5.12* reads — *And by the hands of the apostles were many signs and wonders wrought. Hebrews 2.3-4* tells us of — *... so great salvation ... spoken by the Lord ... confirmed unto us by them that heard him* [that is the apostles]; *God also bearing them* [not everybody else] *witness, both with signs and wonders, and with divers miracles, and gifts of the Holy Ghost.*

Contrary to the impression given by charismatic writers, it is easy to prove that healing miracles wrought by the agency of men were comparatively rare in New Testament times. Readers are invited to establish the point for themselves by a careful reading of the *Acts* narrative. *Acts 9* provides an example of the rarity of these remarkable healings, and the amazement which they therefore generated. We read there of the healing of Aeneas at Lydda, and the raising of Dorcas at Joppa, both through the instrumentality of the apostle Peter. In both cases the event astounded the entire region around and moved many Jewish people to believe in the Lord Jesus as the true Messiah.

The significant point to note is that in each place there was already an established gathering of disciples, yet the apostolic signs were received as a complete 'novelty'. Clearly if the disciples at Lydda were raising up bedridden men like Aeneas every week of the year, Peter's healing act would have gone relatively unnoticed by that region, and would hardly have been recorded as something of quite spectacular importance by Luke.

The only way we can account for the surprise and awe which this event provoked is that it was so unusual. No doubt seriously sick church members often got better (perhaps gradually) in answer to prayer, but a spectacular cure through the agency of a gifted healer was unheard of in those parts — that is the picture which is conveyed by Luke the doctor. Equally, a dead person had never been raised to life by the saints at Joppa because there was no member of the apostolic band in that place. This was obviously a unique occurrence, and this alone explains the great stir in the city, leading to doubting Jews realising that the power of God was with the message of the apostles. Again we say that no one would have been astonished if such miracles had been an everyday occurrence in the early church.

Take the terrible accident which occurred when Eutychus fell from a window in Troas. We do not read in *Acts 20* that all the local gifted healers rushed down to lay their hands on the young man's prostrate body. In fact, so great was the shock, horror and sense of hopelessness among the congregation that Paul's first words as he embraced the corpse were words of comfort to *them*. Where were all the gifted healers volunteering to raise the lad to life? The fact is that there were none, for the only person present who could approach that corpse with any anticipation of a word of healing was a visiting apostle. Why do the charismatic healers offer no explanation of these 'embarrassing' snapshots of the *real* situation in the early churches? We should not let them get away with glib statements about the commonplace nature of sign-miracles — to the confusion of so many young believers — when their scenario is so far removed from the clear record of the book of *Acts*.

The healing gifts were given to the apostles in order that they could be identified and authenticated as genuine bearers of new revelation from God. Any other gifted healers such as Philip, Stephen and Barnabas were people who lived and served 'in the shadow' of apostles. It is possible there were some other helpers besides these three apostolic assistants who were given healing gifts (by the apostles) but *no others are actually named in the Scriptures*. Therefore it is a gross distortion of the record to claim that healings were everyday occurrences in every local church, wrought by the hands of all kinds of believers! Clearly, if there were others (empowered to heal by apostles) there could not have been many, for this would have completely obscured the authentication of apostles, which was the supreme purpose of the healing gift, according to the Bible.

The fact that the healings and miracles were given solely for the purpose of identifying true apostles is stated by Paul in *2 Corinthians 12.11-12*, where he is forced to assert his apostolic office partly because of criticism, and partly because *false apostles* were moving among the churches. To give reassurance and to authenticate himself, he says — *For in nothing am I behind the very chiefest apostles, though I be nothing. Truly the signs of an apostle were wrought among you in all patience, in signs, and wonders, and mighty deeds.*

The authenticating signs of a true apostle were *signs, wonders and mighty deeds.* The *NIV* rendering captures the sense of the original: *The things that mark an apostle — signs, wonders and miracles — were done among you . . .* If numerous 'ordinary' preachers, deacons, or church members had been gifted to perform signs, wonders and miracles, then how would anyone have known who the true apostles were? How would they have known whose words were inspired by God and whose were not? How would they have known which men were the bearers of authoritative revelation and which were imposters?

Dr Rex Gardner, in his book *A Doctor Investigates Healing Miracles*, seems very upset at the possibility that *only* the apostolic band possessed the power to do these things. He is reminded of his missionary days in Uganda where a lay official in the Presbyterian church happened to be the British Governor General. When this eminent man attended church session meetings, he swept up the drive in a beflagged Rolls Royce without number plates, flanked by police outriders. He did this because etiquette demanded that the Queen's representative display appropriate status at all times. Dr Gardner thinks that this is what we want to do with the apostles — merely give them exalted status to establish their claims to leadership. But the point is that they were more than leaders, they were bearers of *revelation*, and thus the Spirit of God pointed to them in a unique way. If He had not done so, the early church would have had no way of knowing which Gospels, letters and other documents were inspired Scripture, and which were merely human ministry, or worse still, false teaching.

Dr Gardner is also worried about the situation which might have prevailed in the church if only the apostles (and perhaps their direct appointees) could perform miracles. He provides a scenario in which one church in a remote, mountainous region has a gifted healer, while other churches do not, and he sees sick people from the underprivileged churches thronging in regular convoys over the mountains to visit the congregation favoured with a healer. This situation he judges to be unbelievable, and therefore turns away from the plain teaching of *2 Corinthians 12.12*. The truth is that Dr Gardner's vision of ecclesiastical chaos would never have arisen for the simple reason that the apostolic gift of healing was not the only way in which God healed sick believers in those days. Somewhere between AD 45 and 50 (at least six or seven years before Paul reminded the Corinthians that healing gifts were signs of apostles) James wrote down what was clearly taught (by inspiration of God) as the *normal* approach to healing for New Testament Christians. *James 5.14-16* will be examined later; it is sufficient for the moment to remind readers that James does not mention gifted healers as the 'norm', but says that praying believers may seek healing blessing directly from God, subject to His sovereign will.

We emphasise that it was comparatively unusual and remarkable for a healing to be administered through the hands (or by the word) of a gifted healer. When this did happen, the sick person was healed *instantly* and often *publicly*, and there was never any kind of relapse. This was a sign-ministry designed by God to mark out the apostles and their accredited helpers, so that the authentic message could be recognised, revered and preserved. (There were other reasons also, which are presented in the chapter — *Proving the Gifts Have Ceased.*)

10. 'Evangelism needs healing miracles'

John Wimber represents the viewpoint of the new extremism well when he claims that signs and wonders were the essential ingredient for success in early church evangelism. He thinks, for example, that Peter received a typical 'word of knowledge' about the duplicity of Ananias and Sapphira, and he insists that present-day Christians should be constantly amazing their worldly friends with similar supernatural insights into their private affairs, sicknesses and sins. Wimber claims that he once saw (in his mind's eye) the word 'adultery' written across the face of a fellow passenger on an airline flight. As he looked, the name of a woman came into his mind and God revealed that He would take the man's life if he did not repent. He further claims that it is by such revelations (ie: words of knowledge) that God means us to startle people in evangelism. Likewise we startle people into believing our message if we can heal, prophesy and cast out demons.

Only a world startled by demonstrations of Christian

clairvoyance and powerful healings will give respectful
attention to the message of the Gospel. By itself the
Gospel is too weak and powerless (in Wimber's opinion)
to break the stubbornness and rebellion of the human
heart. This is the real case for miracles — to supplement
a hopeless weakness in the Gospel itself!

John Wimber's chief example to prove the necessity
of healings and other signs to open up a way for the
Gospel is drawn from the experience of Paul. The usual
extreme charismatic argument is advanced that Paul
failed miserably in his attempt to evangelise Athens
because he used persuasive words unaccompanied by
signs and wonders. Says Wimber, the results were
'meagre'. However, by his next 'stop' — Corinth —
Paul had supposedly learned a hard but mightily significant lesson, namely, that it was vital to combine
proclamation with demonstrations of his supernatural
gifts. The experiment in Corinth proved an astounding
success, and so Paul crystallised this into a kind of
'motto', saying in *1 Corinthians 2.4* — *And my speech
and my preaching was not with enticing words of man's
wisdom, but in demonstration of the Spirit and of power.*

Needless to say, this 'proof text' for the necessity of
healing miracles and clairvoyant insights in the work of
evangelism is typical of the appalling standard of Bible
exposition practised by John Wimber and others of this
school of thought. In a single bound they leap to the
conclusion that Paul's phrase — *in demonstration of the
Spirit and of power* — refers to miracles, and they make
no attempt to check the rest of Paul's statement to see if
he explains himself. If they bothered to read the whole
passage (from verse 17 of the preceding chapter) they
would discover that Paul states very plainly what he
means by a demonstration of power — *For the preaching
of the cross is . . . the power of God (1 Corinthians 1.18).*
Paul goes out of his way to emphasise that the power is

in the preaching, reminding the Corinthians that when he preached to them he concentrated on the preaching of the Cross to the exclusion of all else — *For I determined not to know anything among you, save Jesus Christ, and him crucified* (*1 Corinthians 2.2*).

John Wimber and others not only fail to read the context of their *1 Corinthians* proof text when they twist it to suit their theories, but they also neglect to turn to *Acts 18* where Luke provides a detailed record of how Paul behaved in Corinth. Did Paul give 'words of knowledge' revealing a supernatural awareness of people's private circumstances, illnesses, etc? Did he perform spectacular healings there? Luke is completely silent about such things. According to him, Paul followed *exactly* the same policy that he followed in Athens — he used only preaching — persuasive words — to win souls. First, he *reasoned* in the synagogue and *persuaded* both Jews and Greeks, then he preached to the Gentiles.

The description of Paul's Corinthian ministry given in *Acts 18* contains a phrase which is more clearly translated by modern versions to read thus: *Paul began devoting himself completely to the word* (*Acts 18.5; NASB*). The *NIV* renders the phrase — *Paul devoted himself* EXCLUSIVELY *to preaching* [emphasis ours]. Wimber, however, pictures him going about to amaze people with signs and wonders. According to *Acts 18* Paul's Gentile outreach in Corinth began in a home next to the synagogue, Luke mentioning only the fact that many people heard Paul's words, believed and were baptised. After that, Paul continued in the city for eighteen months — *teaching the word of God among them*. Throughout his account Luke makes no mention of miracles, clairvoyancy, or anything like them.

Paul's opponents knew nothing of these things either, for they voiced only one complaint against him — *This fellow persuadeth men to worship God contrary to the law*.

There is not one solitary word about the things which John Wimber claims — that Paul radically transformed his style of evangelism to one of constant signs and wonders as the result of 'failure' in Athens. However, this is the quality of Bible interpretation which is bound to result when people derive their ideas from supposed 'direct revelations' and then try to find texts to support them as an afterthought.

As it happens, we have good authority elsewhere (*2 Corinthians 12.12*) that the *signs of an apostle* were wrought by Paul in Corinth — *in signs, and wonders, and mighty deeds* — but these were evidently manifested among the band of believers rather than in the public ministry, because Luke makes no mention of them in his account of Paul's public evangelism, and Paul makes no mention of them in *1 Corinthians* where he emphasises that all the evangelistic power was in the Gospel preaching alone. When Paul says (in *1 Corinthians 2.4*) that his preaching was — *not with enticing words of man's wisdom, but in demonstration of the Spirit and of power* — he is making a distinction between preaching which was characterised by a display of *worldly* learning, and preaching which presented God's message. Because he gave no ear-tickling, mind-flattering speeches based on worldly learning, but explained God's way of salvation, the power of the Spirit attended the word preached and hearts were opened and moved. The faith of those converted was not placed in some worldly philosophy, but in the powerful work of Christ in bearing away the penalty of sin on Calvary's cross. It was this Gospel message that had the power, because it is a message about the most powerful accomplishment in the history of the universe — the breaking of the bands of sin by the Saviour of mankind.

Surely we can see how superficial and misplaced the Wimber reading of this passage is! Signs and wonders were always authenticating tokens of apostles in the early days of the church. They were not intended as an ongoing feature of evangelism, for we have all the power that we need when the Holy Spirit works through the proclamation of God's Word. The use of the *1 Corinthians* passage to justify a 'scene' of perpetual signs and miracles worked by all believers is yet another example of how charismatic teachers make wild generalisations based on cruelly shallow handling of the sacred text.

John Wimber says in his *Signs and Wonders* messages — 'After a couple of years of thinking about it I have not been able to find a single case of evangelism which is unaccompanied by the supernatural,'* by which he means a miracle of healing, or a revelation of information from God to the evangelist about the names or secret sins of those listening to them. What right does any preacher have to thunder out dogmatic assertions of this kind when he has obviously made no attempt whatsoever to verifying them from the Bible?** The

Signs and Wonders cassette 1984/8164, no.2.

**The following texts refer to evangelistic encounters which were *not* accompanied by any 'supernatural' event such as a miracle, 'word of knowledge', etc. In *Acts* the evangelistic presentations *without* a miraculous element well outnumber those which were attended by something supernatural. (This list of texts is not exhaustive.)

Acts 5.29-32; 7.2-53; 8.4 & 26-38; 9.20-22; 11.19, 20-21, 22-24 & 25-26; 13.14-43 & 44-49; 14.1, 21 & 25; 15.35; 16.1-5 & 12-15; 17.1-4, 10-12, 16-17 & 18-34; 18.1-6, 7-8, 11 & 19; 19.8; 22.1-21; 23.1-9; 24.10-21 & 24-27; 26.1-32; 28.17-29 & 30-31.

While the Lord Jesus Christ performed miracles of healing constantly, it is noteworthy that many of His great 'evangelistic' statements were not set in the *immediate* context of a miracle (this is true of whole series of our Lord's best-known parables). The following passages illustrate the point:

Matthew 9.10-13 & 14-17; 13.1-53; 16.21-28;
Luke 4.16-27; 7.36-50; 9.57-62; 12.13-34 & 49-59; 13.1-9 & 22-30; 14.25-35; 15.1-32;
John 5.17-47; 6.22-71; 7.11-8.59; 10.1-21.

only response one can make to so many of John Wimber's categorical statements is that they are uninformed nonsense. In this matter Wimber is not merely slightly mistaken, nor even largely in error, he is massively and overwhelmingly wrong, as he is in so many of his emphatic statements about what the Bible teaches.

11. 'The Corinthian church had gifted healers'

Some charismatic healing authors lay great stress on the supposed example of 'body ministry' which was practised in the church at Corinth (according to their reading of *1 Corinthians 12*). They say that the Corinthian church (and therefore, presumably, all the others) had in its membership a full range of spiritual gifts, including healing gifts, so that all the needs of the fellowship could be met. The chapter therefore proves — so charismatic teachers claim — (a) that the gifts were not restricted to the apostles and their appointees; and (b) that many people in every church should be working healing miracles.

However, this interpretation of *1 Corinthians 12* is very wide of the mark because it pays no attention to Paul's clearly stated purpose in writing these words. Paul begins the passage by saying to the Corinthians that he does not want them to be ignorant or in the dark about spiritual gifts. The question is, why would the Corinthians have been *ignorant* or *unaware* of these gifts? After all, if they were experiencing all these gifts they would obviously have had a firsthand familiarity with them! They may have needed instruction or clarification about their purpose and oversight, but they would certainly not have been *ignorant* (Greek: *agnoeo* — to be ignorant).

Quite obviously, therefore, all these gifts were *not* being witnessed in the church at Corinth, and so they needed to have some explanation of these things. Paul tells them about the gifts which were manifested in the church at large, some of which the Corinthians did not possess. Corinth did not have a resident apostle, for example, since the departure of Paul, and yet Paul says grandly — *God hath set some in the church, first apostles, secondarily prophets, thirdly teachers* . . . etc (*1 Corinthians 12.28*). It is quite clear from this that Paul is primarily talking about gifts in the church at large. It is only as the chapter proceeds that he turns his message into a lesson on harmony and co-operation in the local church.

Perhaps the Corinthians were perplexed at the wonderful accounts they had heard about the miracles which had occurred in the church at Jerusalem and elsewhere. At Corinth they had never experienced any-one being struck down dead, as Ananias and Sapphira had been in Jerusalem, and they may never have experienced anyone being raised from the dead either. Perhaps they felt jealous or left out of some of the sign-miracles (though they certainly had their share of signs while Paul was with them). Perhaps they felt inferior because revelatory Truth did not come through some resident apostle of their very own. Paul's purpose in writing this passage was to assure them that they were in no way inferior, but that the limited number of apostles (with their miraculous signs) ministering in the church at large, benefitted the *entire body* of churches.

Sign-miracles performed by (say) apostles in Jerusalem benefitted the church at Corinth (and all the other churches too) because these miraculous gifts authenticated the true messengers of God, thus making the revelation of God sure and certain. No church need be *shaken in mind or troubled* about whether these apostles were truly inspired, or their doctrine authentic or false, because the true messengers of sacred and abiding Scripture received unmistakable authentication. All the people of God therefore benefitted immensely from the certainty and security which was bestowed upon authentic revelation, so that the Word of God could be proclaimed with fitting authority.

Among the gifts mentioned in *1 Corinthians 12* are gifts of healing, and the probability is that these gifts were not present in the Corinthian church either. The basis for this view is, first, the simple fact that the Corinthian letters make no other mention of healers being there. Secondly, Paul provides no instructions about how 'healers' should go about their ministry — a remarkable omission as Paul began *1 Corinthians 12* by telling them that he did not want them to be ignorant about gifts. Such instructions, however, were unnecessary as they had no healers at Corinth.

But does not Paul at the end of this key chapter exhort Christians to covet *all* the gifts? No, he does not. Addressing the whole congregation (not individuals) he exhorts them to *earnestly desire the greater gifts* — the greater gifts being those which convey God's revealed Word, not fleeting signs and wonders. In other words, Paul tells the Corinthians, *as a congregation*, to value each apostolic letter or tested prophetic utterance, and to look forward to such portions of revealed Truth with great anticipation. They must value these above all the sign-gifts, and they must also estimate very highly the teaching ministry which expounds and explains the revealed words of God. Of course Paul does not encourage individuals to be *personally* ambitious to work healing miracles. Rather, he teaches them to realise that the *Word* is vastly more important than the *signs*.

5
Demons, Demons Everywhere!
Where the new 'demonology' goes wrong

CHARISMATIC HEALERS certainly prove the truth of the statement — demons are in the eye of the beholder. It is their opinion that vast numbers of people, both unbelievers and Christians, are seriously or mildly possessed by demons without being even remotely aware of it. Strange to say, the vast majority of traditional evangelical pastors in the West seldom encounter demonic possession answering to the New Testament description (this horrific occurrence being encountered more often in the East). Yet charismatic healers find themselves wrestling with the victims of demons on a daily basis! Either demons are foolish enough to be drawn to exorcists like moths to a light, or these people choose to see demons wherever they look.

The trouble is that the exorcists have developed a confrontational mentality not unlike that of darkest Rome in their attitude to evil spirits. Instead of seeing the spiritual warfare as it is presented in the Bible, where the devil is fought with the weapons of prayer, preaching, witness, godly living, obedience to the Scripture and faith in the promises, these would-be exorcists want to engage in hand-to-hand combat, sensing, seeing and hearing the powers of darkness and striking them with dramatic words of authority. It is a far cry from the picture of the spiritual warfare given by Paul in *Ephesians 6.10-20*. *We wrestle not against flesh and blood* — says Paul — but the charismatic healers seem to want an enemy they can almost touch. They are not content with being engaged in opposing the great power of satanic *temptation* and *influence* but they want to encounter his very *presence* in the form of occupying demons.

Paul does not tell us to attribute countless physical and emotional problems to the presence of a demon literally resident in some part of our being, or to retaliate by aiming a direct verbal assault at this foe. Paul tells us that our struggle is against unseen and generally unknowable powers — the spiritual forces of evil in the heavenly realms (ie: in the celestial sphere). He tells us that we must use God's provided armour and weaponry because these isolate and shield us from direct communication or intimate spiritual contact with the hosts of darkness, while at the same time enabling us to resist the devil's influence and also to wage evangelistic war against him.

Some of the most bizarre statements imaginable are to be found in chapters on demon possession written by authors who have succumbed to the charismatic way of thinking. Here the air is thick with concepts which hang precariously between the superstitions of medieval Rome and the notions of Eastern, pagan religions. John Wimber represents the outlook of many healers when he declares: 'We are called to liberate territory for Jesus Christ, to take back ground from deceiving spirits... As we succeed in this warfare, the victims of Satan's power are released... We must face the enemy; we must fight. Like Jesus Himself, we have a job to do:

proclaim the kingdom of God and *demonstrate* it through healing the sick and casting out demons.'

Other pro-healing writers echo these words, saying that Jesus gave His own authority and power over demons to the disciples so that they (and we also) could exercise the authority of God's reign over the powers of darkness. The basis of this claim is once again the commissioning of the twelve disciples (and also the seventy) when they were sent round the towns of Israel to announce the dawn of Christ's kingdom. We have already considered the fallacy of regarding these unique missions as a pattern for the ongoing work of the church.* The Lord's promise that special signs would follow faithful apostles *(Mark 16)* is also erroneously cited as justification for a ministry of exorcism by Christians today. However, the absence of plausible proof texts becomes most obvious when writers like Colin Urquhart are compelled to fall back on our Lord's words in *Matthew 18.18* — *Whatsoever ye shall bind on earth shall be bound in heaven: and whatsoever ye shall loose on earth shall be loosed in heaven.*

Any reader of *Matthew 18* can see that this is merely 'hit-and-run' Bible interpretation because the words quoted have nothing whatever to do with loosing people from demons. They are about church discipline and how we are to deal with professing Christians who fall into sinful conduct. It is by peppering their prose with such texts as these that the healing authors try to secure credibility for exorcising demons. We need to remind ourselves yet again that they come to these views not primarily by the study of the Bible but by responding to their own thoughts, reflections and dreams as though these were inspired communications from God.

*The Texts Say No!

Can Demons Cause Illness?

What exactly can demons do in the opinion of charismatic healers? It is claimed that they are behind many physical and mental illnesses, and that they enter into people (in varying degrees) so as to control all or some aspects of their lives. Charismatic writers constantly contradict one another in matters of detail, but they all subscribe to some form of demonic residency being possible (indeed common) for Christians also. John Wimber tries to prove that demons may be the cause of many of our illnesses from five Bible texts. These are supposed to show that demons can cause dumbness, blindness, epilepsy, high fever and crippling, but as usual the texts quoted are grossly misused. Three of them are about people who were possessed by demons, and whose physical condition was an outward symptom of their plight.* One of the texts relates to the healing of Peter's mother-in-law and does not mention demons at all! Wimber reads a demon into this text merely because Jesus 'rebuked' the fever. (Elsewhere He rebuked the wind and the waves, so presumably John Wimber believes they can be possessed by demons also.)

The only text quoted by Wimber which could conceivably be taken to show that a demon may cause an illness without 'possessing' the person is *Luke 13.10-17*, where we are told of the woman who was crippled for eighteen years with a *spirit of infirmity*. However, it is fairly evident that this poor woman was demon possessed, for Jesus later described her as one — *whom Satan hath bound*. She was a tied-up prisoner whose awful physical afflictions were a graphic manifestation and reflection of her deeper subjection to demonic captivity. The Gospels distinguish between 'naturally'

*Matthew 9.32; 12.22; Mark 9.14-29.

caused illnesses, and those which were due to demon possession, and there is no biblical basis for the notion that demons are free to cause illnesses outside the context of full demon possession.

The only case in the Bible of a person who suffered from an illness caused by Satan *without* being demon possessed, is that of Job. But in order to afflict Job, Satan had to receive singular permission from God. This surely confirms that the power to inflict illnesses (other than as a consequence of demon possession) is denied to Satan and his demons in the ordinary course of events. Therefore, when charismatic healers dogmatically tell people that certain of their ailments are demonic, they are not acting in line with the teaching of the Bible about what demons can do, nor are they following the example of the Lord Jesus and His apostles. When did they ever treat the illness of a non-possessed person on the basis of it being a demon which needed to be expelled from some particular organ of the body, or from a joint or limb? Such ideas as these abound in pagan religions, but not in the Bible. According to the Bible, illnesses of non-possessed people are not due to the presence of demons in the body, therefore the activity of curing illnesses by expelling demons is a complete nonsense.

How Can We Tell if People are Demonised?

If demons cannot go around occupying *parts* of the body to cause physical illnesses, what about full-scale demon possession of the personality? Are the charismatic healers justified in seeing a demoniac somewhere in every street? On this point all these healers seem remarkably unaware of the basic theological position which has been held by most Christian teachers for generations — namely that the Lord Jesus, at His coming, ended the power of Satan and his hosts to enter and possess souls uninvited. One of the great signs of His coming as Messiah, marking the beginning of the Gospel age, was the profound limitation placed upon the powers of darkness in this respect.

Traditional evangelicals hold that since that time demon possession can only occur where there is some very strong form of invitation or yieldedness to demonic interference, such as yielding to a familiar spirit or interaction with the occult. Gross idolatry, witchcraft, satanism or a lifestyle which is *totally* given over to the pursuit of evil are the factors which may render people vulnerable to demonic invasion according to Scripture, but demons have been barred from entering souls at their whim.* Contrary to this position, all pro-charismatic healing authors proceed on the assumption that the extensiveness of demonisation is now precisely the same as it was in the time of Christ. However, because real cases of demon possession are in practice so hard to find, they have to cheat, moving the goalposts by completely altering the picture of demon possession.

In the Bible, demon-possessed people were variously seized by terrible tantrums or fits, crying out in voices not their own, manifesting extraordinary physical strength, lapsing into insanity, exhibiting clairvoyance, and sometimes becoming deaf, dumb, blind or crippled by the force of their condition. They recognised Christ and His servants and often shrieked out against them. The features of possession were so horrific and obvious that the family of the one possessed was never in any doubt that their relative was truly demon possessed. By stark contrast, John Wimber's 'demonised' people usually suffer symptoms so very different from those recorded in the Bible that he is able to say — 'Most

*See the following chapter for the evidence for this view.

people who are demonised are not aware of it.' It comes as a surprise — even a shock — to their family and friends to learn of it! His description of common symptoms is *nothing like* biblical demon possession!

It is probably to get round the embarrassment of this that Wimber has decided not to use the term 'demon possession' at all, but to opt for the more general term — 'demonised'. This handy piece of new-fangled terminology somehow leaves scope for a broader and more vague concept of demonic activity than is found in the Bible. Having no need to explain why his sufferers do not manifest the biblical symptoms, healers like John Wimber can now point to people on impulse and pronounce them to be 'demonised' by any number of foul spirits.

How can we tell if people are 'demonised'? To what texts does John Wimber (or any other writer) direct us for guidance in making a diagnosis? The answer is — to none. The Wimberite list of symptoms is not taken from the Bible but from his imagination. We are told that a person may be demonised if addicted to drugs or alcohol, or if liable to compulsive lusting, sexual sin, lying, stealing, murder or eating disorders (presumably ranging from gluttony to anorexia).

Equally, one may be demonised if one is in the grip of depression, anxiety, bad temper, self-hatred, an unforgiving spirit, or resentment. Other supposed indications of demonisation include chronic sickness (especially if it runs in the family!), and a disturbed family history involving alcoholism or child abuse. It is claimed that terrifying experiences such as being raped, abandoned by parents or involved in a motor accident may also provide 'avenues' for demons to enter the lives of Christians and non-Christians alike.

Not everyone suffering these problems, we are assured, is necessarily demonised, but many are. Then

how do we know who is and who is not? As always with
John Wimber we are led away from the Scripture,
which seems to him perfectly useless for such things,
and our faith is directed to people (like Wimber
himself) who, as super-gifted wonder-Christians, are
equipped for such diagnostic tasks. Men and women are
needed who possess the *gift of discernment* and who will
have supernatural insight into the sufferer's situation.
They alone can perceive whether or not the sufferer is
demonised. In head-on collision with all this, Bible
passages such as *Matthew 4.24* and *8.16* show that real
demon possession was so unlike 'ordinary' diseases
(either of body or mind) that it was easily recognisable
and distinguishable.

Can Demons Possess Believers?

John Wimber teaches that born-again Christians can
come under the control of demons in many areas of
their lives, but he is so hard pressed to prove his point
that he even has to classify King Saul as a believer. His
'symptoms' — fits of anger, murder, fear, witchcraft
and suicide — were apparently all signs of a demonised
believer! Saul is, of course, a major Old Testament
example of unbelief and disobedience to the Lord;
certainly not a person in whose heart there was any
work of grace. Even Judas has to be pressed into service
as a believer (Wimber forgets he was described as *the son
of perdition*) in the desperate search for examples of
demonised Christians in the Bible. Peter, alas, is labelled as temporarily 'demonised' simply because the Lord
said — *Simon, behold, Satan hath desired to have you,
that he may sift you as wheat*.

When Wimber claims that Christians risk being
'turned over to Satan' (demonised) if they persist in
unconfessed sin, he gives the example of Ananias and

Sapphira to prove his point, but while these two certainly succumbed to powerful temptation from Satan, there is no word in *Acts* to the effect that they were *demonised*. In the event they were held fully and personally responsible for their sin, for at no time were they out of control in the sense that a demon was in the driving seat of their lives. Besides this, the idea that they were demonised implies that Peter took quite the wrong course of action in rebuking them so sharply. He should have done what a disciple of John Wimber would have done and commanded the demon(s) to leave. He should have used his 'kingdom authority' (as these writers call it) in obedience to the alleged command of *Mark 16*. How different the book of *Acts* would look if the apostles had acted in accordance with the teaching of today's extreme charismatics.

John Wimber descends to the realm of the ridiculous when he tells us that Christians may be unknowingly demonised because demons inherited from their parents have never been cast out. Even he cannot bend a biblical text to fit this notion and is obliged to seek support from the practice of the third-century Roman church which submitted all new converts to the rite of exorcism in order to filter out evil spirits.

Some charismatic healers recoil from the idea that Christians can be demonised, but whatever terms they use, at the end of the day they all teach that demons can invade the soul or body of the believer in some form. Colin Urquhart, for instance, says that Christians cannot be *possessed* but they can be *oppressed*. However he is only playing games with words because he teaches us that 'oppressing' fiends must be commanded to depart and release their hold. His formula is that they should be ordered out — 'and the oppression broken in the name of Jesus and by the power of His blood'.

Colin Urquhart offers no more guidance than John

Wimber as to how believers may know if they are oppressed by a demon. All he can say is that 'it feels as if you are in a cage or prison and need to be set free; or a great cloud of heaviness has descended on you and you find it extremely difficult to praise God or to pray.' As such an experience is not necessarily produced by demons, how can we be certain when it is, or when not? The great problem of diagnosis arises once again, but Mr Urquhart cannot solve it. Sadly we are left entirely at the mercy of our subjective imaginations — or at the mercy of those people who supposedly possess a gift of discernment. Imagination is lord!

These writers obviously cannot suggest any *biblical* guidelines for diagnosing demon possession or oppression of believers because the Bible says absolutely nothing about demons oppressing believers. Nor does the Bible say that demons should be ordered out 'by the power of the blood', as Urquhart argues. Indeed this primitive formula for exorcism is the kind of thing that vampire stories are made of, only instead of a vampire being frightened away by light reflected off a silver cross, a demon is frightened away by a Christian shouting out a sentence containing reference to the name and the blood of Jesus.

Roman friars in the dark ages grew fat by turning the blood of Christ into a magic formula, and many an exorcist is exercising a thriving ministry by a strikingly similar means today. The blood of the Lamb is not to be used as an incantation or charm to frighten away demons. *Revelation 12.11* tells us that the saints overcame the devil *because* the blood of the Lamb covered them, not because they shouted it out like a magic spell. Also, they overcame because of *the word of their testimony* and their selfless loyalty to the end.

In the case of Christians who come to believe that they are demonised or oppressed, most charismatic authors say that self-exorcism can be achieved without recourse to other helpers, but the tragic consequences of these ideas in the lives of believers are all too easy to predict. Imagine the demoralising effect upon many sick or depressed people when they are told that their problems are due to demons. And what if they strive to command the demon out of their lives, only to experience no recovery or relief? Imagine the agony and perhaps also the terror of having to conclude that a demon still has a deep hold upon them! Or what about believers who, by perverse escapism, duck out of taking personal responsibility for their sins by blaming them on to demon oppression?

What about the comfort and consolation wrenched away from troubled believers because the protective promises of God are smashed to pieces by this theory that demons from hell can get right into their personalities notwithstanding that their bodies are temples of the Holy Spirit? Clearly, Christians do have to engage in a great struggle against the wiles and temptations of the devil, but nowhere in the New Testament is temptation resisted by a process of commanding demons to loose their hold and leave a Christian's mind or body. Satan is resisted by being denied success in the temptation. Or if he mounts an attack of depressive suggestions, he is resisted as the believer strives to keep hold of the comfort and promises of God's Word.

When James says, *Resist the devil, and he will flee from you,* he tells us that this is done by drawing near to God, cleansing our hands, purifying our hearts, experiencing mourning and weeping for our sins, and humbling ourselves in the sight of the Lord so that He may lift us up. James says nothing about ordering away the demon(s) by the blood of Jesus, and neither does any other New Testament writer. How do charismatics explain the fact that the Lord seems to have kept His church waiting

2,000 years for modern 'apostles' to supplement the teaching of the Bible?

It is utterly impossible for any demon to co-occupy with the Holy Spirit the body or soul of a genuine believer. Says Paul, *What? know ye not that your body is the temple of the Holy Ghost which is in you, which ye have of God, and ye are not your own? (1 Corinthians 6.19).* Once truly converted, the indwelling Holy Spirit will never leave us, for we have the Saviour's promise to this effect: *And I will pray the Father, and he shall give you another Comforter, that he may abide with you for ever; even the Spirit of truth . . . for he dwelleth with you, and shall be in you (John 14.16-17).*

Charismatic authors often appeal to Paul's words in *2 Timothy 2.26* about people who are in the snare of the devil, having been taken captive by him. These people are thought to be believers who have somehow become possessed by demons, but anyone reading the passage will see that this is not so. Paul says that the Lord's messengers must be apt to teach — *In meekness instructing those that oppose themselves; if God peradventure will give them repentance to the acknowledging of the truth; and that they may recover themselves out of the snare of the devil, who are taken captive by him at his will (2 Timothy 2.25-26).*

It should be clear that the people in view here are obstinate resisters of the Gospel who need to be saved. It should also be apparent that they are not demon possessed anyway, but simply doing Satan's bidding by responding to all his temptations, as so many worldly people do. There is a vast difference between succumbing to Satan's temptations and being demon possessed!

Demon possession of true believers in Christ is a theological impossibility, and this includes the brand of possession which Urquhart and others call 'oppression'.

Should We Address Demons Today?

We could spend considerable time commenting on many major contradictions between leading healing authors, but one example will suffice — the procedure for casting out a demon. Some writers insist that the exorcist must first find out the names of occupying demons (eg: Wimber — 'I never call anything a demon until I have actually talked with the demon . . . I say: In the name of Jesus, I command you, spirit, tell me your name.') However, another leading international healer and exorcist says that this is both absurd and unnecessary, asserting that as long as one simply takes authority over the demons one ought to be able to command them out instantly. All long prayers and any investigation of the names of demons is considered pointless.

The real truth is that all these teachers are utterly wrong in their ideas because God has forever forbidden verbal interaction between His people and demons. Apart from the sign ministry of exorcism practised by Christ and by the apostles as His immediate representatives (which was designed to authenticate His divine power and to assure us that *He* has power over demons) no *direct* intercourse between believers and demons is permitted or prescribed in the New Testament.

Deuteronomy 18.10-12 is one of several absolute prohibitions of *every conceivable form* of involvement or commerce with evil spirits. God says: *There shall not be found among you anyone who . . . uses divination . . . practices witchcraft . . . interprets omens, or a sorcerer, or one who casts a spell, or a medium, or a spiritist, or one who calls up the dead. For whoever does these things is detestable to the Lord (NASB).*

We must clearly understand *why* it is so heinously wicked to approach evil spirits. It is not *only* a matter of turning away from God and trusting in someone or something other than God. It is primarily because any attempt at direct contact with (including conversation with) an evil spirit is detestable to the Lord. The principle behind this prohibition is that direct communication with demons by human beings is a most vile and offensive act in the sight of God, regardless of the purpose or motive. The Hebrew word translated *detestable* (*abomination* in the *AV*) means loathsome or disgusting. Demons are loathsome, evil spirits full of hate, deceit, subtlety and deadly danger. We are absolutely forbidden to pry, enquire, interrogate or interact with them in any way whatsoever, no matter what the circumstances may be, and no matter how 'good' our intentions.

It may help convey the point if we imagine the reaction of parents who, having taken their toddler into the countryside, suddenly spot the child about to explore a stream of foul sewage. In this case, it is the *nature* of the stream that provokes the abhorrence and alarm of the parents, not the motives of the child. A single demon from the abyss represents an evil force millions of times more loathsome and dangerous than any amount of sewage. In the sight of God *any* direct communication between His children and the spirits of darkness is an abomination. Misguided charismatics who want to locate demons in order to interrogate them, show how little they grasp the unfathomable vileness and subtle power of these spirits.

One of the offenders listed in *Deuteronomy 18.10-12* is called a *medium* (*NIV*, *NASB*). The Hebrew term covers any level of communication with a spirit, ranging from asking a spirit's name to conducting a seance. Another offender is called *a spiritist* (*wizard* in the *AV*). This refers to a 'knowing one' or a clairvoyant person. Yet many charismatic healers strive desperately to 'perceive' unseen knowledge about people and events.

What they call 'words of wisdom and knowledge' (perverting biblical terms) are no different from the clairvoyant impressions of ancient spiritists!

Even worse, modern charismatic workers will often try to get 'insights' into the identity and intentions of demons which they think may be present in suffering people. Some of these workers are no doubt cheap pretenders who invent all their so-called insights. But others who believe very deeply in their theological system strain every nerve to become open and sensitive to the unseen world of demons, little realising that God condemns all such activity as spiritism. Countless profane and superficial Christian exorcists strut round the Christian world impressing the weak-minded with their knowledge of and power over evil spirits. Some may be lying showmen. Some may be genuine workers who are just caught up in a welter of imagination and hysteria. (When such people really do encounter a genuine case of demon possession they get a terrible shock!) But some exorcists doubtless *have* managed to penetrate the spirit world to some degree, and they have become 'knowing ones' or spiritists — detestable in the sight of God because they have touched forbidden things. It is utterly impossible for a spiritist to be on the Lord's side, for spiritism in *all* its forms is deeply loathsome to God.

To look at the matter from another angle, what are people saying if they think that they can enter into *direct* engagement with demons and survive undefiled? They are revealing how little they understand the exceeding sinfulness and the terrible power of demons. They are saying that they rate them as less dangerous than human criminals, for those would-be exorcists would probably shrink from tackling an armed raider or a night-time burglar. Notice the bravado and composure which characterises charismatic exorcisms! Why, demons are nothing at all! A dozen or two can be expelled in ten minutes, and then they can preach a sermon as though nothing had happened.

What are the exorcists saying to God when they take on the world of wicked spirits with — as it were — their bare hands? They are telling the Lord that they do not need the Son of God and the holy angels to represent them in the arena of unseen spiritual strife. They do not need a divine Representative, a sovereign Protector, a Shield and Defender to protect them from the powers of darkness and from *direct* exposure to the devil and his hosts. They can go out against the foe, cross his battle lines and peer into his marshalled ranks. The exorcists have rewritten the basic doctrines of the Bible, declaring to God that they no longer need to be 'in Christ' for the spiritual warfare. How strong they are! How capable!

Only the Lord Jesus can rebuke and cast out a demon, and we must never dare detract from His priesthood! Believers must not be taken in by these ideas that they may have power and authority to recognise, address and command demons. If we ever find ourselves confronted by a clear case of demon possession answering to the horrifying signs given to us in the biblical record, then we must resort to the ministry of prayer and, as opportunity arises, we must exhort the demon-possessed person to go to Christ, the only Mediator between God and man, for salvation and deliverance. We cannot accomplish either of these things ourselves; we must always send people to Christ.

This is what preaching is about — it is the process of sending people to Christ for *all* their spiritual needs, because we cannot fulfil any of them. Charismatics have adopted not only the thinking of pagan cults, but the priestcraft of Rome in imagining that mortal men possess the delegated power of Christ over the fiends of darkness. The terrible truth is that the advocates and exponents of exorcism are the very people who are most likely to be at risk from demonic interference, and this is doubtless a prime reason why God forbids presumptuous experiments in this area. A host of men like John Wimber regularly defy the Lord's command by seeking interaction with demons. At the same time they lay aside their rational minds and yield themselves to the government of random thoughts and imaginings, supposing that this will bring them words of wisdom and knowledge. These are the very people who sooner or later encounter *real* demons or familiar spirits, and who, because of their experiments with occult techniques and spirit manipulation, are cruelly exposed to demonic power.

One wonders how many of these extreme charismatics have been people who, while deluded about their salvation, moved arrogantly into a ministry of exorcism only to come under exploitation by a familiar spirit. Would this not account for *some* of their clairvoyant insights hitting the mark? Does this not explain how their signs and wonders (like the signs and wonders of false prophets and pagan cult priests today) *sometimes* seem inexplicably real? Satan and his demons have a certain amount of power over the natural realm and can imitate physical healing, give rise to clairvoyancy, levitation, telekinesis, and certain other signs and wonders (*2 Thessalonians 2.9*). Is it not possible that some of these charismatic healers could themselves be demonised?

Some charismatic 'proof texts'

Here are some further examples of Scripture passages misappropriated by John Wimber and other leading healers to prove that our ministry today should include a constant stream of exorcisms. Readers are invited to take note of the gross misuse of these texts.

1 Timothy 4.1: Now the Spirit speaketh expressly, that in the latter times some shall depart from the faith, giving heed to seducing spirits, and doctrines of devils. These words make no reference to demon possession, nor to the casting out of demons. They describe perverse but perfectly rational people who teach doctrines which (probably unbeknown to them) are invented and suggested to the minds of infidel scholars by demons.

1 Peter 5.8-9: Be sober, be vigilant; because your adversary the devil, as a roaring lion, walketh about, seeking whom he may devour: whom resist stedfast in the faith. This passage is about resisting Satan's various temptations. It tells us that we do this by keeping up our spiritual duties, and says nothing about casting out demons.

John 20.21: As my Father hath sent me, even so send I you. The reasoning applied to this verse is this: just as Jesus was sent by the Father to achieve a variety of objectives — including the casting out of demons — so we are now sent to carry on all aspects of His ministry. However, the reasoning is obviously superficial and false, because the Saviour did many things which we cannot do, and which we must not attempt to imitate. He came, for example, to display His divinity and to die on Calvary; things which we cannot do. Our Lord's words in *John 20* are intended to assure us that we have a divine commission for our work. They do not for a moment imply that *every* ministry and action of the Lord is to be emulated by us.

6
Demons Cannot Occupy At Will
Six scriptural reasons

EVANGELICALS OF BYGONE YEARS advanced powerful biblical arguments for the view that widespread demon possession was ended by the ministry of Christ on earth. Since then, our forebears maintained, demon possession can only occur when people voluntarily expose themselves to demonic activity, as in the pursuit of spiritism. In recent years, however, pro-charismatic writers who are unfamiliar with traditional evangelical theology on this matter have stated dogmatically that there is no biblical evidence to support the traditional view.

Six arguments in favour of the old evangelical position are presented here, with supporting Bible passages. In the mind of this writer, any one of these is sufficient to sweep away all the man-made notions of charismatic exorcists. Taken together, these arguments would seem to be nothing less than invincible.

1. The Lord Taught That Demons Would Be Restricted

The Lord Jesus Christ Himself equated His casting out of demons with a curbing of Satan's activity from the beginning of the Gospel age. In *Luke 11.20-22* He said — *If I with the finger of God cast out devils, no doubt the kingdom of God is come upon you. When a strong man armed keepeth his palace, his goods are in peace: but when a stronger than he shall come upon him, and overcome him, he taketh from him all his armour wherein he trusted, and divideth his spoils.*

In these words the Lord describes the Old Testament period during which the devil was like a strong man armed, with vast areas of the world in his keeping. The devil's goods were 'in peace', so that nations stayed in spiritual darkness and any demons which occupied people remained unmolested. There was no successful or lasting exorcism achievable by anyone. Then the Lord described His own coming with the finger of God, casting out demons as a sign that He was the true Messiah and that the Gospel age had begun. His great onslaught upon the hosts of darkness (which came to its climax on Calvary) would end the freedom of Satan to blind the nations. In overcoming Satan our Lord took away his armour — the steel bands around nations — and handed those people over to the possibility of Gospel influence.

The power of demons to occupy individuals indiscriminately must logically be included in this curbing of Satan's power, because it is exactly like his work of deceiving the nations. In deceiving the nations Satan and his demons seize the minds and hearts of people, obstructing all spiritual influences. When a demon occupies an individual it is the same activity in microcosm. It is as though the demon has built a wall around that person, just as Satan built an impenetrable wall of paganism round entire nations in Old Testament times.

By contrast the New Testament description of the devil since Calvary is that of a humbled fiend. No longer can he take over nations or individuals at will.

He must, like a spiritual vagrant, live in the streets and gutters, tempting people from outside. His power continues to be hideous and great, because the hearts of people are desperately wicked on their own account. They are strongly prejudiced in favour of believing his lies and acting on his temptings. However, he can no longer take them over and inhabit them *at his will*. The only remaining possibility for demons to occupy souls since Calvary, is where people have consciously and wilfully co-operated with demonic influences, and yielded up their lives to them.

This binding or restraining of Satan is also seen in *Mark 3.27* where the Saviour describes His action against Satan in these words: *No man can enter into a strong man's house, and spoil his goods, except he will first bind the strong man; and then he will spoil his house.* Satan is most certainly active as an evil tempter, but being a vagrant rather than a lord he must now secure the co-operation of his victims. As the 'prince of the power of the air' he has no palace, no throne and no rights. He and his demon hosts are wandering fiends, living by their 'wits'.

The Lord Jesus Christ again equated the casting out of demons with the curbing of Satan at Calvary, saying — *Now is the judgment of this world: now shall the prince of this world be cast out (John 12.31)*. Satan was cast out chiefly through his defeat at Calvary, but he was also 'cast out' at the time of Christ in respect of his power to occupy human beings *at will*. This last activity must be included in the words of Christ — for the Lord used the very words *(cast out)* which describe an exorcism.

The first argument supporting the cessation of involuntary or widespread demon possession is that the Lord Jesus Christ clearly taught that His ministry on earth brought a severe curtailment of Satan's powers to possess souls.

2. David and Paul Say the Demons Are Now Limited

The second argument is derived from Scripture passages which both predict and explain the captivity of demons which began at Calvary. *Psalm 68* is a prophecy, looking forward to the coming of Christ into the world, His conquest over the powers of darkness, His ascension into Heaven, and His rule over His Church throughout the Gospel age. The apostle Paul quotes the psalm in this sense.

Psalm 68 opens with the words — *Let God arise, let his enemies be scattered: let them also that hate him flee before him.* The Messiah is coming, and the devil's hosts shall flee before Him. They will flee during His earthly walk (as He casts them out of individual people) and they will flee in their hordes when He gains the victory on Calvary.

When the Saviour ascends into Heaven (says the psalm) He will receive gifts which He will pass on to men:— *Thou hast ascended on high, thou hast led captivity captive: thou hast received gifts for men; yea, for the rebellious also, that the Lord God might dwell among them.*

The question is — who are these captives and what are the gifts? The answer is given by Paul in *Ephesians 4.8* and *11* (his 'commentary' on *Psalm 68*) — *When he ascended up on high, he led captivity captive, and gave gifts unto men . . . And he gave some, apostles; and some, prophets; and some, evangelists; and some, pastors and teachers . . .*

Having defeated Satan on Calvary, our Lord ascended, and like an ancient conqueror He led away a host of captives. He stripped many powers from the demons of darkness, and took from them 'spoil', which He distributed to His own followers. What 'spoil' could our Saviour have taken from the devil and his hosts which would have been suitable for giving to the followers of

Christ? Before Calvary the devil and his hosts held vast influence over humanity. They did not hold it by right, because they had stolen it. Nevertheless, they wielded irresistible power to deceive the nations, to keep the Gentiles in darkness, and to occupy souls in great numbers.

At Calvary Christ took that away from the devil and his hosts, and after His ascension He gave it instead to His Church. He stripped the demons of their *unfettered* power over the minds of people, and gave to His disciples the irresistible power of His Word, and of Gospel ministry.

So the hosts of darkness, Satan and his demons, are dispossessed of a great area of power, and in exchange, great influence is given to New Testament believers, who are given the gifts of Gospel communication with which to penetrate all the deceived nations of the world.* The devil and his hosts are not altogether removed from the scene as yet, but they cannot shut the Gospel out of nations, nor thwart the process of conversion to Christ, nor occupy people without their consent. *Irresistible* power over the soul is one of the 'spoils' of Calvary.

3. The Demons Knew of Their Demise

The third group of Scripture passages which leads us

---

*Some exegetes hold that the captives represent the people of God, who (through Calvary) were defeated as rebels and taken in train by Christ as His *glorious* captives. However, the language of *Psalm 68* describes bitter enemies who are taken in train as a humiliated foe. Paul makes a similar statement in *Colossians 2.15*, speaking again of Christ's victory over the devil and his angels at Calvary:— *And having spoiled principalities and powers, he made a shew of them openly, triumphing over them in it.* The 'spoil' which God took from the devil and his hosts was the influence and 'territories' they had seized. These God 'gave' to His Church, so that the Gospel might be preached throughout the world.

to believe that involuntary possession by demons cannot take place today, tells how demons reacted to the Saviour. The demons themselves seemed to know that the ministry of Christ would bring a great change in their activities, and terminate their power and liberty to occupy countless souls at whim. The man of Gadara (who had been possessed for a long time by many demons) on seeing Jesus — *cried out, and fell down before him, and with a loud voice said, What have I to do with thee, Jesus, thou Son of God most high? I beseech thee, torment me not (Luke 8.28).*

Jesus had commanded the unclean spirits to come out of the man, and they realised with terror and alarm that their freedom to occupy human beings at their whim had come to an end. It was because they knew that they would never be permitted to occupy another living person that they pleaded to be sent into the swine. Thus, even the demons gave testimony to the fact that 'involuntary' demon possession was terminated by the ministry of Christ.

The demon-possessed man in the Capernaum synagogue, when he saw Christ, cried out saying — *Let us alone; what have we to do with thee, thou Jesus of Nazareth? Art thou come to destroy us? (Mark 1.24)* There was definitely only one unclean spirit in this man, but it spoke as representing the anguish and apprehension of *all* its fellow demons. This foul being expressed not only its own fear at being cast out of occupation, but spoke for its whole 'side'. A parallel account of this event is recorded in *Luke 4.33 36.*

4. Satan Cannot Manifest Himself Openly

A fourth argument which supports the view that Satan and his demons are now restricted from occupying people, is the fact that God has declared that He will restrain Satan from revealing himself. He has been placed under a powerful restraint so that he cannot be incarnated, nor even manifest himself in his appointed *man of sin* until the Lord permits, and that will be immediately prior to Christ's return in glory. Such a restraint would, of course, be rendered utterly ineffective if demons were free to occupy large numbers of people at whim, and thus express their 'demonic' behaviour through them. This would represent a massive, open manifestation of Satan's hosts in the world. Obviously the curbing of Satan must include a similar restriction upon his demonic hordes.

In *2 Thessalonians 2.6-7* the apostle Paul describes how Satan's representative is prevented from arising until God's time arrives: *And now you know what is holding him back, so that he may be revealed at the proper time. For the secret power of lawlessness is already at work; but the one who now holds it back will continue to do so till he is taken out of the way (NIV).* So Satan's self-manifestation is strictly limited until his final 'little season' — *And then shall that Wicked be revealed, whom the Lord shall consume with the spirit of his mouth, and shall destroy with the brightness of his coming (2 Thessalonians 2.8).*

During this present age the devil is forced to maintain a low profile in the pursuit of his strategy. It is by secrecy and stealth that he promotes false religion, atheistic philosophy and the gods of gold and silver — materialism and secularism. He is forced to remain invisible in his operations. Even when Satan is set at liberty for his 'little season' (shortly before the return of Christ) he will not be permitted to become incarnate, or visible. By subtle manipulation of society he will bring a great falling away or apostasy; a period of extreme rejection of God and all moral laws. (Other passages of Scripture such as *Revelation 19.15-21* also refer to Satan's proxy-manifestation and the destruction of the *man of sin* at the end of time.)

In summary, Scripture rules out the ostentatious display of demonic personality seen in widespread demon possession. Satan's present activities must be carried on by subtlety and stealth, and demon possession on a widespread scale is hardly subtle or secret. Demon possession is therefore a real but rare occurrence today.

5. The Bible Defines Demonic Activity

The fifth argument against widespread demon possession occurring today is that various New Testament passages tell us precisely what Satan's activities will be during the Gospel age, and the occupying of people is never included in such passages. The tragic irony is that while charismatic teachers perspire and struggle to dislodge demons (which are mere figments of their imagination) the *real* demons have succeeded in infecting their churches with worldliness and false teaching. According to the Word of God the role of demons today is to tempt people to sin, to persecute and try the people of God, and to spread false doctrine.

We read, for example, in *1 Timothy 4.1: Now the Spirit speaketh expressly, that in the latter times some shall depart from the faith, giving heed to seducing spirits, and doctrines of devils.* Most commentators agree that *seducing spirits* refers to lying, hypocritical people who are the instruments of the devil. *Doctrines of devils* should be translated — *doctrines of demons.* Demons are now actively engaged in inventing and propagating doctrinal lies. They linger in seminaries, Bible colleges and in theological faculties at universities — anywhere where they can find vulnerable clergy and ministers.

James 3.14-15 informs us that demons, far from occupying people, are engaged in stirring up trouble between church members. He says: *If ye have bitter envying and strife in your hearts, glory not, and lie not against the truth. This wisdom descendeth not from above, but is earthly, sensual, devilish* (literally: demonic, or, of demons). How easily we can be deceived by demonic temptation. As church members we can so easily be carried away by ill-feeling and resentment towards one another. We fail to remember that jealousy, anger and bitterness are all suggested and stimulated by lingering demons.

In *1 John 4.1-6* we are told — *believe not every spirit* — because demons are always at hand, always ready to suggest some carnal policy which is in complete contradiction to the Word of God and the principles of obedience and faith. While charismatics worry about demon possession, these demons are busy promoting ecumenism, worldliness, pop-idiom worship, love of luxury, careerism, and loose behaviour among Christian people.

We conclude that while the devil and his hosts no longer possess the power to occupy anyone (without their deep co-operation), they themselves are behind the current mania to locate and cast out imaginary demons, because this latest novelty diverts the attention of Christian people from the real activity of demons — hurting and polluting Christ's churches. *Revelation 2.9, 20, 24* and *3.9* are other verses which show that demons are behind all hypocrisy, false worship and false doctrine.

Revelation 12 sets out the strategy which humiliated demons will follow throughout this present dispensation. Will they occupy people at will? No, replies *Revelation 12*. Knowing that their time is short they will vent their spite upon the churches of the Saviour. For how long will they do this? For the whole of the Gospel age, as we see in *verse 17*, where the dragon is depicted making war with the remnant of the seed of the woman — the people of God — to the end of time.

Once we see that this is the teaching of the New

Testament we can grasp what a disastrous and tragic thing it is for true believers to be drawn aside by the topic of demon possession. Those who become obsessed with exorcisms are 2,000 years behind the times. They have failed to notice the very precise list of demonic activities provided in the New Testament.

6. No Biblical Authority for Exorcism

The sixth argument against widespread demon possession occurring today is the total absence of any positive instruction to believers in the New Testament about exorcism. The apostles (and the seventy special messengers) received power over demons solely because they were announcing that the kingdom of God had arrived. In other words, the casting out of the demons was the signal for the coming of Christ and the inauguration of a new, Gospel age.

The disciples' ability to cast out demons was never intended to be a continuing feature of Christian service, and accordingly, no instructions are included in any New Testament book about how they should be cast out. None of the classic passages which deal with our warfare against the devil say a single word about demon possession or exorcism. Though the apostle Paul covers all the deep affairs of the spiritual warfare, he omits any reference to demon possession and exorcism (eg: *Romans 6-8, Galatians 5-6, Ephesians 6.11-18*).

Is it conceivable that a *commonplace* spiritual tragedy would have been left out accidentally? Of course not, for the Bible is fully sufficient for all our needs. There are no instructions about how to deal with demon possession because it is a comparatively rare event, and one which is covered by the normal rules of evangelism.

Let us suppose a rare case of demon possession presents itself. First, we must remember that our commission is to proclaim the Gospel, not to exorcise the demon. Secondly, we remember that the Lord has warned that without conversion, exorcism would be useless anyway. Whether a person is demon possessed or not, the only scriptural way for that person to be saved is to repent and believe the Gospel. There can be no different procedure for a demon-possessed person.

What about after conversion? Is it possible that a demon-possessed person could be saved, and then need an exorcism to cast out the demon? The answer is that this is theologically inconceivable. What kind of conversion would it be if the occupying demon was not dislodged and cast out by the Spirit of God as He entered in and took over the life?

If any Christian worker is ever confronted with a case of demon possession (presumably someone deeply involved in the occult) then that Christian worker's role is to witness, to pray, and to urge the possessed person to apply to Christ for help and salvation. We must never 'play priest' and try to take over Christ's role. Only Christ can expel a demon, just as He alone can forgive sins and renew a life. As Luther said — 'We cannot expel demons with certain ceremonies and words as Jesus Christ and the apostles did . . . We cannot ourselves expel the evil spirits, nor must we ever attempt it' (*Table Talk*).

Exorcism In the Name of Jesus

All this leaves one query unanswered. If there are no instructions for an ongoing ministry of exorcism in the Bible, what about the apparent example of the apostle Paul when he turned to the demon-possessed girl at Philippi and said, *I command thee in the name of Jesus Christ to come out of her (Acts 16.18)*? Should we not use the name of Jesus to cast out demons today? The very definite answer is — no; under no circumstances must we abuse the name of Jesus and use it like a lucky charm or superstitious formula for waving at evil spirits.

When the apostle Paul used the name of Jesus, he did not do so because the utterance of the name contributed anything! He was announcing to all who were present that he cast out the demon *on the express authority of Christ*. As an apostle he had been personally 'licensed', authorised and empowered by Christ to cast out demons. We are not apostles, and we have not been authorised or empowered to do this. Our great commission does not authorise us to cast out demons. Paul was able to say that he did this by the authority of Christ as a commissioned apostle. We cannot say that, and so we must never use the name of Jesus.

Whenever something is done (in Scripture) *in the name of Jesus* it means that it is done *by His express command and on His behalf*. When Paul writes to the Corinthians *(1 Corinthians 5)* he tells them that Christ has directed him to command them to expel their immoral member. He therefore commands them — *in the name of our Lord Jesus Christ*. Always the term — *in the name of Jesus* — means that Christ has commanded something. Something is being done on His behalf and for Him. We receive children in Christ's name because He has expressly commanded us to do so. We gather for prayer in Christ's name, because we are obeying His express command.

The Lord Jesus cast out great numbers of demons before Calvary, but some were left in temporary occupation of people so that the apostolic band could cast them out also. Thus *Mark 16.17* would be fulfilled, and it would be known to all that the apostles truly were the representatives of Christ. As far as we are concerned, we must never use the name of Jesus as a magic key for something which He has not commanded us to do.

7
Proving the Gifts Have Ceased
Bible statements on revelatory and sign gifts

ONE OF THE STRANGEST ASPECTS of the current charismatic debate is the fact that many *non*-charismatic people are unwilling to say categorically that certain gifts have ceased. Indeed, some claim that there are *no biblical grounds* for saying that these gifts have ceased, and they regard those who do say so as rather extreme in their views. The viewpoint which teaches that the revelatory gifts and sign-gifts have ceased has come to be called 'cessationism' — a term which somehow suggests a modern minority opinion; an *'ism*! This is certainly a very strange turn of events because 'cessationism' used to be the universally accepted position among evangelicals of all denominations and traditions, the prevailing judgement of Bible-believing people throughout church history.

Until a few decades ago, practically every preacher, church officer and well-taught believer could have explained the biblical basis for the passing of apostles, prophets, sign-miracles and tongues-speaking. We have come to a very sad state of affairs when the historic viewpoint is regarded by some as 'extremism', and its advocates are accused of being antagonistic to a living experience of the Spirit of God. Such ideas are utterly unrealistic as the finest periods of church history testify. In times of great awakening and wonderful outpourings of the Spirit the leading instruments of revival have been *cessationists*! The most spiritual and challenging sermons and books to be found in the archives of great Christian literature come from *cessationists*.

In his book *Signs of the Apostles*, Walter Chantry brings together quotations from many great names of church history, all of them standing clearly for the cessationist position. He cites 'Fathers' such as John Chrysostom and Augustine. He draws on the Puritans Thomas Watson and John Owen. He provides succinct statements by Matthew Henry, Jonathan Edwards and George Whitefield. James Buchanan, Robert L. Dabney, George Smeaton, Abraham Kuyper, W. G. T. Shedd, C. H. Spurgeon and Benjamin Warfield are also quoted in support of the cessationist position, ably representing the overwhelming majority of evangelical preachers and scholars of their day. A. W. Pink equally insisted on the cessation of the gifts. We could add to Chantry's list Reformers such as Luther and Calvin, and a host of other great names of history.

It hardly needs saying that all these servants of God believed passionately in the continuation of the *felt* power of the Holy Spirit in the lives of individuals and churches. None of them were dry formalists; all pressed the necessity of a Christian life manifesting all the power and assurance of the Holy Spirit. Interestingly, none of the worthies just mentioned was a dispensationalist, a point which demolishes the oft-repeated charismatic claim that cessationism is a product of dispensationalism. We repeat that it was the *standard* teaching on the gifts of the Spirit long before dispensationalism rose to its present popularity.

If we were to add to the historic list of cessationists all the great names of the dispensational tradition it would become even more obvious that cessationism was the only viewpoint on this subject seriously held by our evangelical forebears. So, let us at least be clear on this point — cessationism is *not* merely the opinion of a minority of obscurantists and pedants; it is the view which has been held by the overwhelming majority of evangelicals until this present age of unprecedented doctrinal decline.

To avoid any confusion it is necessary to point out that the historic 'cessationist' position does *not* say that miracles have ceased, but that the *revelatory* and *sign* gifts have ceased, that is, the power to speak inspired words, and the power to work miracles and perform healings. God no longer delegates the dispensing of miracles to human agents.

God is always able to do mighty things when and where He pleases and no one doubts that He wonderfully overrules events, circumstances and human biology to bring His purposes to pass. Every Christian can testify to the Lord at times answering prayer to bring things to pass in a way which was wholly unexpected and inexplicable. The issue is not whether God is willing to answer the prayers of His people and to do remarkable things for them, but whether *sign-miracle workers* and *gifted healers* are with us today.

James 5 shows that God invites us to pray for restoration from sickness, warning us, however, that the Lord *may* have an *end* or purpose in an illness, so that it *may* have to be borne patiently. If God does grant a healing blessing we may never know whether He chose to sanctify the medical treatment, or to work in a direct way to bring about recovery. Nevertheless we will believe that the Lord has blessed us even though we have no indisputable, empirical proof of the fact. Healing blessing is not for convincing unbelievers about the things of God; it is a personal blessing for those who trust the Lord. In our day it is not given as a sign-miracle to authenticate apostles, neither is it a means of boosting our faith. Perhaps one of the reasons why God allows us to suffer some of our illnesses is to prevent us from perverting the blessing of healing into a miracle-tonic which takes the place of genuine faith in the Lord and His Word.

Cessationists, therefore, believe that the Lord still intervenes in a direct manner in the lives of His saints in many wonderful ways, but that He no longer gives to individual people the power to work miracles. Charismatic writers, by contrast, constantly claim that there is no text in the Bible which plainly and categorically states that gifts of prophecy, healing and tongues will cease. They also claim that cessationists rest their entire position on a single passage of Scripture — *1 Corinthians 13.8-10* — the precise meaning of which is hotly debated. All this is very misleading, because there are many passages of Scripture which show that the gifts would cease with the passing of the apostles. Furthermore the great names of church history who have held this view have hardly ever quoted *1 Corinthians 13* to support their argument. Because this chapter is so controversial we shall set it aside entirely and confine ourselves to all the other passages which prove that certain gifts have ceased.

Where, then, are the texts which plainly say that revelatory gifts and sign-gifts would cease? The first answer is that they are to be found in passages which tell us what the *purposes* of the gifts were. Let us imagine that our government decides that the internal combustion engine will be banned by a certain date, after which no car, bus or truck may be powered by petrol, and only battery-driven vehicles will be permitted.

Imagine further, that 500 years after this event, a university researcher tries to determine exactly when the petrol pumps closed down. He spends months examining government records to find the date for the banning of roadside pumps, but finds nothing. Once he is satisfied that no legislation to ban the pumps was ever passed, he concludes that they remained open for a couple of centuries after the disappearance of petrol-driven vehicles.

Such a conclusion would be absurd, because the banning of petrol-driven vehicles would *automatically* lead to roadside petrol pumps becoming extinct. No special legislation would be needed to close the pumps. Without a *purpose* to serve, the pumps would inevitably and automatically become redundant. So it is with the gifts of the Spirit. If the *purpose* for which any gift was given was a temporary purpose, then that gift would obviously become redundant once its purpose was fulfilled. Therefore, the key question in deciding whether any gift was intended to continue is — What was the *purpose* behind the gift?

We should not look for a categorical statement saying, 'Such-and-such a gift will cease,' but we should look for texts which tell us whether the *purpose* behind that gift was short-term or enduring. The following purposes or objectives behind the gifts are revealed in the Word of God, and it will be seen that in many cases these objectives were fully achieved during the age of the apostles, proving that some of the gifts had no further purpose to serve.

1. Apostles Were Unique Witnesses to Christ

We shall consider first the gift of apostleship and the sign-gifts possessed by the apostles. Apostles were given to testify to the life and resurrection of the Lord and to be the inspired channels of new Truth. We shall take first their special role as witnesses of the life and resurrection of Christ. A crucial family of texts (ignored by charismatic writers) is that which teaches that the apostles were given unique power to perform sign-miracles *expressly to establish their credibility as eyewitnesses of the risen Lord*. These powers were given only to a select group of men who (a) were chosen by Christ, and (b) had seen the risen Lord. Miracle-working powers were not given generally to all preachers in the early church, nor even to *all* the people who had seen the Lord after His resurrection.

The apostles are repeatedly described as *witnesses*, the Greek word referring to judicial witnesses in a court of law. The disciples were not witnesses in the sense that we are Gospel witnesses today, but in a much greater sense, for they 'gave evidence' that they had actually seen the Lord after His resurrection. The texts we are about to quote will prove that the gift of *apostleship* had a short-term purpose because the apostles were a select, exclusive band of *eyewitnesses* of Christ. These are the verses which prove the point:—

In *John* 15.27 we are told how the Lord Jesus appointed the eleven to this special task: *And ye also shall bear witness, because ye have been with me from the beginning.* He reminded them of this before His ascension into Heaven, when the risen Lord said to the disciples: *Thus it behoved Christ to suffer, and to rise from the dead the third day . . . And ye are witnesses of these things (Luke 24.46-48).* The Lord also told the disciples *when* they would receive their unique gifts to function as witnesses: *Ye shall receive power, after that the Holy Ghost is come upon you* [Pentecost]: *and ye shall be witnesses unto me (Acts 1.8).*

Acts 1 confirms that the apostles were specially chosen by the Lord and trained for their task as witnesses to His resurrection. Luke tells us how the Lord gave instructions — *unto the apostles whom he had chosen: to whom also he shewed himself alive after his passion by many infallible proofs (Acts 1.2-3)*. Eleven apostles are then named as having witnessed these *proofs* and also the ascension of the Lord Jesus into Heaven *(Acts 1.13)*. Soon, under the guidance of the Spirit, a twelfth apostle was appointed, the required 'qualifications' being set out. He had to be someone who had been with the Lord and His disciples since the baptism of John and who was an eyewitness of the resurrection. Having found those qualified, the definite choice of the Lord was necessary, for every apostle was appointed by the Lord.

The special role of apostles as witnesses of the resurrection is repeatedly emphasised by the apostles themselves. When Peter preached on the Day of Pentecost he stood up *with the eleven* and said, *This Jesus hath God raised up, whereof we all are witnesses (Acts 2.32)*. Peter again stated his role as an eyewitness when he preached by Solomon's Porch about — *The Prince of life, whom God hath raised from the dead; whereof we are witnesses (Acts 3.15)*. He referred yet again to his role as an eyewitness when summoned before the council. Speaking of Christ he said, *Him hath God exalted . . . And we are his witnesses of these things (Acts 5.31-32)*.

Much later, preaching to a gathering of Gentiles in the house of Cornelius, Peter said — *And we are witnesses of all things which he* [the Lord Jesus] *did both in the land of the Jews, and in Jerusalem . . . him God raised up the third day, and shewed him openly; not to all the people, but unto witnesses chosen before of God, even to us, who did eat and drink with him after he rose from the dead. And he commanded us . . . to testify (Acts 10.39-42)*. Could any passage state more plainly than this the fact that apostles were a select band of eyewitnesses, personally chosen by the Lord?

The apostle John also drew attention to an apostle's unique task of witnessing to the physical reality of Christ's life and resurrection in *1 John 1.1-3*, saying — *That ... which we have heard, which we have seen with our eyes, which we have looked upon, and our hands have handled ... (for the life was manifested, and we have seen it, and bear witness) ... that which we have seen and heard declare we unto you.*

All these texts show that the first and highest duty of the apostles was to be eyewitnesses of the majesty of Christ; to give evidence to their generation, and to set down their testimony in writing for posterity. Once we grasp the paramount importance of this, and the fact that these apostles were all specifically chosen by Christ, then we will realise that the apostles could never have successors.

Paul was added to that illustrious band of apostles by a special appearance of Christ to him. He had not walked with Christ as the twelve had done, but he saw the risen Lord, and received a unique commission from Him to be an apostle. God sent Ananias to say to him, *The God of our fathers hath chosen thee, that thou shouldest know his will, and see that Just One ... For thou shalt be his witness unto all men of what thou hast seen and heard (Acts 22.14-15).* Paul later said — *Am I not an apostle? ... have I not seen Jesus Christ our Lord? (1 Corinthians 9.1).* In listing the appearances of the risen Lord, he says — *And last of all he was seen of me also, as of one born out of due time (1 Corinthians 15.8).* Since Paul, no person on earth has seen the risen Lord and therefore there can be no further apostles.

It passes understanding that the leaders of some charismatic groups have the temerity to regard themselves as 'apostles' in our day! Can they say with Paul, 'Have I not seen Jesus Christ our Lord'? Have they met the risen Lord? Of course not; their definition of what makes an apostle is simply not from the Bible. Such modern 'apostles' reveal their fundamental ignorance of the significance of biblical apostles, and of their chief task and purpose!

But what of the sign-miracle gifts which are also claimed by many these days? According to the Bible the original purpose of these gifts was to authenticate apostles to show that their testimony was true. Without some form of attestation the people might well have regarded the eyewitnesses of Christ as madmen, but the Holy Spirit gave them the gift of healing and the gift to work miracles so that the seal of God was clearly upon their evidence. One of the chief purposes, therefore, of the sign-gifts was to verify the witness of the apostles to the life and resurrection of Christ, as we see in Luke's record in *Acts 3-4*. Notice how their witness to the messiahship and resurrection of Christ is stressed in this passage.

Peter and John had been preaching in Jerusalem, frequently mentioning the resurrection of Christ (*Acts 3.13, 15, 21* and *26*). As a result the Jewish authorities arrested them — *being grieved that they taught the people, and preached through Jesus the resurrection from the dead* (*Acts 4.2*). When a hearing was convened before the high priest at the Jewish council, Peter stayed loyal to his special duty as an eyewitness of Christ, and referring to the lame man healed by him, he boldly stated — *Be it known unto you all . . . that by the name of Jesus Christ of Nazareth, whom ye crucified, whom God raised from the dead, even by him doth this man stand here before you whole (Acts 4.10).*

The council released Peter and John, forbidding them to speak about the name of Jesus. But they returned to the disciples and prayed for boldness of speech and for the continuing power to do signs and wonders. The answer to their prayer is recorded in a verse which makes it very plain that these signs and wonders were expressly intended to authenticate *the apostles* as eyewitnesses of the resurrection. Luke writes: *And with great power gave the apostles witness of the resurrection of the Lord Jesus: and great grace was upon them all (Acts 4.33).*

We need to remind ourselves of the other texts in *Acts* which also say that these sign-gifts were peculiar to the apostolic band (the apostles and two or three deputies who showed some of their power). *Acts 2.43* and *Acts 5.12* both say that the signs and wonders were exclusive to the apostles.

In *Hebrews 2.3-4* the link between the eyewitness role of apostles and the sign-gifts is spelled out in unmistakable terms as the writer speaks about the apostles who personally heard the words of Christ — *God also bearing them witness, both with signs and wonders, and with divers miracles, and gifts of the Holy Ghost*. Here the sign-miracles are expressly described as authenticating signs for apostles. Furthermore, the writer of *Hebrews* points back to those sign-miracles as events which belonged to the past, because by the time this epistle was written (the late 60s AD) the ministry of apostles (including sign-miracles) had apparently already passed into history.*

In spite of the biblical emphasis on all this, we consult charismatic books in vain for any information about the special role of apostles as witnesses, or about the *purpose* of their personal, authenticating signs. Most healing writers seem to think that the purpose of sign

---

Mark 16.20 also firmly relates the *signs following* to the work of the original apostles, using the past tense to describe their two-fold ministry (ie: of the Word coupled with signs). In the Greek the indicative verb-form governing the entire sentence is in the past tense — *preached*. Most evangelical scholars favour a late AD 60s date for *Mark*.

miracles was simply to 'confirm' in a vague and general manner the ministry of the early church and to create a pathway for faith in the unbelieving heart. They do not trouble to take note of the precise details given in the Bible. It is extraordinary that writers who set themselves up as specialists on the gifts of the Spirit should reveal so little knowledge of what the Bible teaches about the *purposes* behind the gifts.

All the texts just quoted prove that a select band of apostles (including Paul) were given an exclusive task to perform for which they were uniquely qualified. It was because they were eyewitnesses, giving evidence of the teaching and resurrection of the Lord, that they received authenticating powers from the Spirit. Like witnesses in a court of law they testified to the things that they had seen and heard, and God confirmed *their* witness with signs following. With the passing of those chosen eyewitnesses the sign-miracles also passed away, for their work was done and their purpose fulfilled. How can miracles continue to authenticate eyewitnesses when no eyewitnesses are left on earth? The 'trial' is over; the witnesses have been heard; the verdict has been given; the witnesses have been dismissed; the result now stands in the records.

May people possess sign-miracle gifts today? The question we must ask is — What was the biblical purpose of those gifts? The answer is — it was to authenticate and vindicate Christ's appointed eyewitnesses. Are there chosen apostles today? Are there eyewitnesses of His majesty still living? The authentication of chosen eyewitnesses is the primary purpose of sign-miracle gifts, and clearly it is a purpose which was fully accomplished during the lifetime of the apostles.

2. Sign-gifts Attended New Revelation

The sign-gifts were also given to the apostolic band to signal that new revelation — New Testament Scripture — was being given, and to personally authenticate the inspired penmen. The apostles were not only eye-witnesses of the ministry and resurrection of Christ, they were also channels of new revelation, a momentous function which obviously needed to be endorsed by the Holy Spirit in signs, wonders and mighty deeds so that people might know that their words carried the authority of God Himself.

At a practical level the people needed to be able to distinguish between the apostles and uninspired, 'ordinary' teachers of God's Truth. They also needed to be able to discern false apostles, and so the true spokesmen were given authenticating power to work sign-miracles such as spectacular healings. The best-known text teaching this is *2 Corinthians 12.12* where Paul reasons with those who doubted his apostolic office, saying — *Truly the signs of an apostle were wrought among you in all patience, in signs, and wonders, and mighty deeds.* The Corinthians could be sure that Paul really was inspired by God because of his sign-gifts. They could tell quite easily that he was not just an ordinary (uninspired) teacher of God's Word, but a genuine penman of new Scripture.* *Hebrews 2.4* makes the same point when it tells how the apostles spoke the word of Christ — *God also bearing them witness* with sign-miracles.

The attestation of inspired penmen by signs and wonders was nothing new, because from the beginning of the Old Testament the Lord used this method of signalling that He was speaking Scripture to His people.

*Some penmen of New Testament books were not apostles, but the authenticity of these penmen and their Scriptures was attested by apostles.

Various passages in *Deuteronomy* provide ample evidence of this. In *Deuteronomy 4.34-36* Moses reminds the people of all the signs and wonders they had seen — the outstretched arm of the Lord — validating the revelation of Himself to them. Moses declares — *Out of heaven he made thee to hear his voice*. In *Deuteronomy 6.22-24* Moses again speaks of the Lord showing signs and wonders before revealing His statutes to Israel and commanding their obedience.

The final 'epilogue' chapter of *Deuteronomy* pays tribute to the outstanding stature of Moses as a prophet of God *whom the Lord knew face to face* on account of all the signs and the wonders which the Lord sent him to perform in mighty power (see *Deuteronomy 34.10-12*). God's prophet, as the channel of revealed Truth, was mightily authenticated by these signs. Throughout the history of Israel rare but recurring episodes of signs and wonders continued to be associated with the bearers of inspired messages. In *2 Kings 5* we get a telling insight into this with the healing of Naaman's leprosy. A captured Israelite maid wished that Naaman, her master, could be seen by Elisha the prophet — *for he would recover him of his leprosy*. When he eventually heard of Naaman's illness Elisha exclaimed — *Let him come now to me, and he shall know that there is a prophet in Israel*. Elisha knew well enough that his 'powers' were given for the express purpose of accrediting his office as a channel of God's Word.

At times when there was no divinely inspired teacher in Israel, then pious members of the population would become very cast down and say to themselves — *We see not our signs: there is no more any prophet (Psalm 74.9)*. After four centuries of silence between Old and New Testaments, the Lord granted a fresh burst of revelation, signalled in the familiar manner with signs, wonders and mighty deeds. On the Day of Pentecost the new converts knew that it was safe to continue *stedfastly in the apostles' doctrine* because *many wonders and signs were done by the apostles (Acts 2.42-43)*.

Once the period of revelation was complete and the New Testament was completely delivered, the authenticating signs were no longer relevant. Indeed, had they continued, they would have caused disastrous confusion because believers would have expected new books of the Bible to appear! They would have looked for new apostles and prophets. The *purpose* behind the sign-gifts tells us that these gifts were temporary ones. When the apostles passed, and the last book of the Bible was in place, then the *signs of apostles* passed also.

Perhaps the most *direct* and categorical text confirming the passing of the sign-gifts is *Revelation 22.18: For I testify unto every man that heareth the words of the prophecy of this book, If any man shall add unto these things, God shall add unto him the plagues that are written in this book*. Because revelation is complete and is no longer 'in process', it obviously follows that the *signs* of revelation are also no longer 'in process'.

3. Signs Marked the End of an Era

Another purpose of the sign-gifts was to mark the end of the Jewish age and the beginning of the Gospel age. The sign of tongues-speaking was the first 'wonder' to be manifested in the life of the newly-formed Christian church on the Day of Pentecost. Peter stood up before the amazed crowds in Jerusalem to declare that the prophecy of Joel was being fulfilled in their sight, and that tongues — along with the miracles which soon followed — were *signs* from God that He was doing a new thing. Joel had prophesied that a time would come when God would pour out His Spirit upon all mankind (ie: the Church would no longer be pre-eminently

Jewish, but international; *Joel 2.28*). This would be marked by the occurrence of ordinary people speaking messages by the inspiration of God. The outbreak of tongues-speaking, according to Peter, was the exact fulfilment of Joel's words.

Joel also foretold a display of wonders to mark the beginning of the 'age' during which the Holy Spirit would extend the Church throughout the world. In quoting *Joel*, Peter uses the word *signs*. All these things — miracles, wonders, tongues — were *signs* which pointed to a great change and a new era being ushered in. Sign-miracles and tongues placed a very obvious divine seal of approval upon the new order.

Imagine the effect on the Day of Pentecost when the people of Jerusalem were alarmed by the sound of a rushing mighty wind seemingly approaching from the heavens. As it moved into the city this great disturbance of air settled, not in the Temple — thought to be the valid focal point of worship and Truth — but in an upper room where the disciples of the Lord were gathered. Upon *them* the Spirit descended, and to *them* was given the ability to speak and preach in languages which they had never learned.

Signs, wonders, and tongues were God's signal to the population of Jerusalem (swollen by visitors) that a new day had dawned, that the mantle of God's blessing had passed to a new community, and that a new order had arrived. These tongues came as a shock and a salutary warning to crowds of proud, cynical Jews, many of them being moved to enquire into the things of God, saying, *We do hear . . . the wonderful works of God . . . What meaneth this? (Acts 2.11-12)*. Why would the Lord give the Jews a sign at all? Why all these sign-miracles and tongues to impress upon them that His presence was with a new church order? If unbelievers are not given special sign-miracles today, why should the Lord have given them to the Jews? Did God owe the Jews special proofs and indications of His actions?

The answer is that the Lord did, in a sense, 'owe' the Jews a clear, supernatural signal to validate the new order. After all, the Jews had been trained over many centuries to cleave to the law of God as given to Moses and to be rigorously loyal to the detailed ceremonial delivered by him. They had been trained to preserve and obey every jot and tittle of the law of that dispensation. But now that Christ had fulfilled the law and broken the ceremonial yoke, inaugurating the priesthood of all believers and bringing in a new and living way, Jews needed some highly auspicious sign that these things were from God. The *pious* Jew might well be perplexed at having to abandon the manner of worship which God had given, and the *godless* Jew may well have hidden behind his concept of an unchanging Mosaic order, making it an excuse for rejecting the Gospel. So, when God swept away the old and brought in the new, He did so with a fanfare of tongues-speaking, signs, wonders and mighty deeds, all of which had been foretold by Joel of old.

Paul confirms to us that the fundamental purpose of the gift of tongues was to provide the Jews with a sign that the divine presence had passed from the Jewish theocracy to the international Church of the Lord Jesus Christ. In *1 Corinthians 14.21* he quotes *Isaiah 28.11-12*, saying — *In the law it is written, With men of other tongues and other lips will I speak unto this people* [the Jews], *and yet for all that will they not hear me, saith the Lord.* Paul shows that this prophecy was fulfilled in the gift of tongues, adding — *Wherefore tongues are for a sign . . . to them that believe not.* First and foremost tongues were designed to prove something to a specific people, namely, the Jews. They were intended to challenge and provoke the unbelieving Jewish masses to realise that the new Christian community truly had the Lord with them, whereas the traditional Jewish 'church' had no current evidence of the divine presence.

Tongues also spoke eloquently of the international nature of the new church, showing that it would henceforward be a multiracial, multilingual church, whose members had a responsibility to speak God's Word to people of every land and nation. God was showing very graphically that the glory had departed from the Temple, and settled upon the disciples of the 'Sect of the Nazarenes'.

Tongues had precisely the same sign value when they were given to the group of Gentiles gathered in the house of Cornelius at Caesarea, some eight years after Pentecost. As Peter preached, the gift of the Holy Ghost was poured out upon these Gentile converts and they spoke in tongues. The result was that — *they of the circumcision which believed were astonished* and Peter said, *Can any man forbid water, that these should not be baptized, which have received the Holy Ghost as well as we? (Acts 10.45 and 47.)* The sign which had previously spoken to Jews in Jerusalem, proving that God was with the new Christian church, spoke again to Jews — this time Jewish believers whose minds were prejudiced against the entry of Gentiles into the Christian church. By means of 'other tongues' God signalled to the Jewish Christians that Gentile believers were totally accepted by Him, and were in the church on an equal footing with Jews.

When Peter told the Jerusalem church what had happened at Caesarea, he used words which suggest to us that tongues-speaking had not occurred very much during the eight years since Pentecost. He said: *As I began to speak, the Holy Ghost fell on them, as on us at the beginning. Then remembered I the word of the Lord, how that he said, John indeed baptized with water; but ye shall be baptized with the Holy Ghost (Acts 11.15-16)*. The ability to speak in a foreign language was possibly not very widely given once it had made its original impact on the crowd of Jews in Jerusalem. It was probably given in some measure to the Gentile believers of Corinth on account of the Jewish community there, and the constant traffic of Jewish merchants and travellers through this major trading city.

The commentator Matthew Henry states the purpose of tongues-speaking in these words: 'The gift of tongues was one new product of the spirit of prophecy and given for a particular reason, that, the Jewish pale being taken down, all nations might be brought into the church. These and other gifts of prophecy, being a sign, have long since ceased and been laid aside, and we have no encouragement to expect the revival of them; but, on the contrary, are directed to call the Scriptures the *more sure word of prophecy*, more sure than voices from Heaven; and to them we are directed to take heed, to search them, and to hold them fast.'

Is the purpose of tongues as a *sign* fulfilled? Of course it is, because the event which the sign attested lies in the distant past. If the sign of tongues was still given, great confusion would result because it would indicate that God was even now effecting a great transition from one order to another! The inaugural signs for the Lord's 'change of step' have served their purpose, and to seal matters the Temple of the Jews has long since been destroyed, and the sacrifices ended. Like the sound as of a rushing mighty wind and the cloven tongues like as of fire, the sign of tongues and the sign-miracles have done their work and have retired from the scene.

4. The Gift of Prophecy an Interim Ministry

What about the gift of prophecy? Was this given to

serve a temporary or an ongoing purpose? The gift of prophecy served to help teach the people of God in the absence of a completed Bible; therefore it was a gift given to the church to service a *special* and *temporary* need. We know this because New Testament prophets are generally listed right next to apostles (eg: *1 Corinthians 12.28; Ephesians 2.20; 3.5* and *4.11*) indicating their similar (though inferior) status as recipients of direct inspiration, and their membership of an equally temporary order. While some prophets were inspired to write Scripture,* their normal ministry was less exalted.

Through prophets the Lord spoke upbuilding words to congregations which did not yet possess all the Scriptures. They functioned alongside the ordinary teachers, often combining both offices (eg: Judas and Silas, *Acts 15.32*). There were not very many in each church if *Acts 13.1* is a reflection of the normal 'staffing' of an early Christian congregation. At Antioch (a very large church) there were five *prophets and teachers* ministering when the Holy Spirit sent two of that number (Saul and Barnabas) away on missionary service, leaving only three. Prophets were not usually attested by signs and wonders (for the texts limit these signs to the apostles and their appointees). They sat together on the 'platform' in a church service and checked the veracity of each other's messages (*1 Corinthians 14.30* and *32*).

Prophets are included with apostles as being part of the foundation stage of the Church of Jesus Christ in *Ephesians 2.20* — *built upon the foundation of the apostles and prophets*. The prophets referred to here are unquestionably New Testament prophets.** Because prophets

*Mark, Luke, James and Jude (half-brothers of the Lord) and the writer of *Hebrews* were prophets who were inspired to contribute to the written Scripture.

**William Hendriksen argues thus: (1) Apostles are mentioned first. (2) The *foundation* in *Ephesians 2.20* is of a dwelling shared are *foundational* gifts, we are not to expect them in the 'superstructure' period of the Church. Nowhere in the New Testament is there any guidance or command about how to discern or appoint prophets because, like apostles, they passed from the scene with the completing of the Bible, which is held forth as fully sufficient for all our needs. The idea that God is giving inspired words to prophets today is a total contradiction of the absolute sufficiency of Scripture, and of many Bible passages which categorically state that revelation would be completed and ended within the ministry of the apostles.*

The *Baptist Confession* drawn up in London in 1689 expresses the traditional convictions of Bible Christians perfectly in these words:

'Therefore it pleased the Lord at sundry times and in divers manners, to reveal Himself, and to declare His will unto His church; and afterward, for the better preserving and propagating of the Truth, and for the more sure establishment and comfort of the church, protecting it against the corruption of the flesh and the malice of Satan and of the world, to commit the same wholly unto writing; which maketh the Holy Scripture to be most necessary, those former ways of God's revealing His will unto His people being now ceased ... The whole counsel of God concerning all things

equally by Jew and Gentile. (3) In *Ephesians 4.8-11* prophets are again mentioned *after* apostles, and these are definitely gifts bestowed on the church by the ascended Christ. (4) In *Ephesians 3.5* Paul uses precisely the same phrase, making it clear that he means *New Testament* prophets who have just received revelations alongside apostles.

This — according to Dr Hendriksen — 'would seem to clinch the argument in favour of New Testament prophets'. (See Hendriksen's *New Testament Commentary, Exposition of Ephesians*, page 142.)

*John 16.13; 2 Thessalonians 3.6; 2 Timothy 3.16-17; Jude 3 and *Revelation 22.18-19*. (See note on Agabus at the end of this chapter.)

necessary for His own glory, man's salvation, faith and life, is either expressly set down or necessarily contained in the Holy Scripture; unto which nothing at any time is to be added, whether by new revelation of the Spirit, or traditions of men.' *(Baptist Confession I:1 and 6.)*

Gifts Which Continue

The charismata or spiritual gifts which have an ongoing place in the life of the church are *evangelists, pastors, teachers, helps* and *governments* — in other words, the teaching, pastoring and leading ministries of the church. This is plain, first, from the fact that unlike other gifts the purpose of these gifts was not fully discharged and fulfilled in Bible times, as the great commission and numerous other scriptures show.

Secondly, the New Testament expressly provides for the continuation of these gifts (unlike the others). The pastoral epistles, for example, tell us the qualifications of teachers and leaders, and include strong exhortations to go on preaching the Word. Paul gives the clearest instructions about the continuation of teaching and leadership roles when he tells us how we ought to conduct ourselves — *in the house of God, which is the church of the living God, the pillar and ground of the truth.* But nowhere in the pastorals does he tell us to perform healings or other sign-miracles, or to expect prophetic inspiration and so on.

What the Gifts Did Not Signify

The reason why charismatic writers expect sign-gifts like healings and tongues to continue is that they fail to take note of the purposes of God in giving these gifts, and they substitute their own ideas about what the gifts achieved. They imagine that the sign-gifts were given in order to startle people into believing, and to provide a help or prop for faith. Clearly if these were the objectives of signs, then there is no reason why they should not continue. Why should the Lord give advantages to the churches of the first century which were to be denied to all subsequent centuries of Christian witness? However, the sign-gifts were *not* given to create or to boost faith, but to give the very specific signals and authentications which we have identified, with supporting texts, in the preceding pages. The pro-charismatic writer Dr Rex Gardner provides us with an example of writers on this subject who overlook the biblical reasons as to why the gifts were given. He says: 'They are gifts to the body of Christ for everyday use.' But the many texts we quoted earlier do not agree; they insist that most of the gifts had very specific sign-tasks.

Miracles and healings still occur today, by the power of God, and in answer to prayer. But sign-miracles wrought through the hands of gifted individuals, for the purpose of authentication, belong to the age of the apostles. They never were given to serve as a means of strengthening faith for the ongoing centuries, and we should take careful note of the words of Christ to doubting Thomas — *Thomas, because thou hast seen me, thou hast believed: blessed are they that have not seen, and yet have believed (John 20.29).* John's Gospel goes on to record: *And many other signs truly did Jesus in the presence of his disciples, which are not written in this book: but these are written, that ye might believe . . . (John 20 30-31).* The signs are not being displayed today, because we have the signs of Christ (and the apostles) written in the Lord's book, and it is by reading or hearing of what is written that we shall come to believe in Christ, and shall have life in His name.

Does Galatians 3.5 refer to miracle workers in the congregation?

The question is asked — Does not *Galatians 3.5* imply that people other than members of the apostolic band were working miracles on a regular basis? The text reads:— *He therefore that ministereth to you the Spirit, and worketh miracles among you, doeth he it by the works of the law, or by the hearing of faith?* (The *He* at the beginning of the verse refers, of course, to God.) This verse if read superficially certainly gives the *impression* that miracles were being regularly seen among the Galatian Christians.

However, we should be aware that the Galatian epistle was written very soon after Paul had himself been ministering among them (note the words — *so soon* — in *Galatians 1.6*). If we accept the so-called 'South Galatian' scenario (supported by most evangelical scholars) then Paul either wrote this epistle in AD 48, less than a year after his ministry there, or in the middle of his second missionary journey only a few months after his second visit to them (recorded in *Acts 15.40-16.8*).

Either way the Galatians had experienced very recently Paul's own sign-miracles. Since his departure, the church had allowed itself to be influenced by Judaising teachers, but neither they nor the ordinary Galatians could work sign-miracles. Therefore Paul challenges them to remember that their recent experience of sign-miracles was exclusively connected with his own ministry — the apostle of justification by faith alone.

Agabus and Other Prophets

Questions are often raised concerning the case of Agabus (*Acts 21*) who did not merely prophesy doctrinal and exhortational messages, but who also foretold the future. Does this not indicate that prophecy went beyond the task of teaching the people in the absence of a completed Bible? And what about the daughters of Philip who were prophetesses? As they presumably could not preach in the church, is it possible that their prophecies were also something other than teaching and exhortation?

The case of Agabus does not contradict or weaken in any way the position that prophets received doctrinal and exhortational matter directly from God to teach to the people only so long as the Scriptures were still incomplete. Certainly, the way Agabus was listened to shows that believers were well used to such prophets foretelling events. But this should not surprise us, for we simply learn that the Old Testament rule for the attesting of a true prophet still applied. How could God's people be sure that brother Agabus should be recognised as a teacher of 'prophet status'? The answer is, that at times God inspired him to *fore-tell* as well as to *forth-tell*. The first kind of prophetic word served as a means of personal authentication, so that the second kind of prophetic word could be trusted by the people.

The fact that Philip had four daughters who were prophetesses should not trouble or concern us either. Though they would not have been able to preach or prophesy in the mixed gatherings of the church, they would doubtless have taught, admonished and counselled among the women. Also, there is evidence of a highly developed ministry to the young in the churches of those days, based on the concept of the Jewish synagogue schools.

Interestingly, the prophecy of Agabus in *Acts 21.10ff* was about something which was soon to be incorporated in the Word of God. He gave word of the imprisonment of Paul, later to be inscripturated in the record of Luke and several epistles. Though it may seem that he was only addressing a contemporary situation, it is noteworthy that he was *perfectly* fulfilling the role of (New Testament) prophets by delivering God's Word in advance of a completed Bible!

8
Implementing James 5
Directions for divine healing which charismatics ignore

CHARISMATIC AUTHORS ought to be highly embarrassed by the teaching of James because the procedure which he lays down for healing prayer outlaws and invalidates virtually every one of their healing methods. This is especially significant when we remember that *James 5* is the *only* passage in the New Testament which addresses clear and binding instructions about healing to 'ordinary' Christian people. All other references to healing simply *record* the unique, authenticating sign-miracles of the Lord Jesus Christ, His heralds (the twelve and the seventy) and the apostolic band. In none of these references is there any commission or command to other Christians to attempt to heal in the same way.

James 5, written as early as AD 45-50, stands alone as a directive to Christians who do not possess the rare, first-century gifts referred to by Paul as — *the signs of an apostle*.

We may be sure that the rules laid down by James were carefully complied with by the congregations of New Testament times, unless a member of the apostolic band happened to be on the scene to bestow a healing sign-miracle. Today these rules must continue to govern our response to sickness in our churches.

Because of the confusion created by present-day healers we must first note how *James 5* utterly excludes from church practice all the popular features of charismatic healing. To begin with, the idea of an itinerant healing ministry is excluded because James requires that sick believers be ministered to by the elders of their own church. The command is perfectly clear — *Let him call for the elders of the church*. Nowhere does James say that we may choose some alternative way of seeking help, such as waiting for the next famous healer who visits our town.

The idea that God has placed 'gifted' healers in our local churches is also excluded by James, who says nothing about sending for someone who possesses a gift. We are simply to send for the elders, whose task is to *pray*, not to effect the healing by virtue of some personal gift. Indeed, James goes out of his way to say that if a sick person is raised up this will be by the power of the Lord working in answer to prayer, not by any power channelled through the elders.

The *James 5* passage also excludes the convening of special public healing meetings or sessions. It provides only for bedside gatherings* arranged at the request of the sick person. Healings performed in specially convened rallies by specialised healers cannot be fitted into the simple scheme laid down by the Holy Spirit through the words of James.

James is also silent about the exercising of clairvoyant powers and the receiving of 'words of knowledge' popularised by the non-evangelical faith-healer Kathryn Kuhlman and now employed by charismatics everywhere! He says nothing about the gathered elders

---

*And — of course — private prayer (*James 5.16*).

receiving a 'TV picture' in their minds of diseased organs, and so these practices are disqualified by the silence of Scripture. We read *James* in vain if we are looking for all the extraordinary trappings of charismatic healing. The ungarnished procedure of *James* 5 stands in total contrast to all the antics of modern healers, and thus condemns them all as misguided and unbiblical.

Should the elders at the bedside command a disease to leave? Of course not, because they are not said in *James* 5 to possess any executive power over disease whatsoever, nor are they told to utter grandiloquent commands in the name of Jesus. John Wimber tells us that when he was called to visit a very sick baby in hospital he addressed the 'spirit' of death saying, 'Death, get out of here!' Immediately, he claims, the atmosphere changed. James, however, has never heard of such amazing feats being achieved by men, and so he fails to give this spectacular kind of role to the elders of the church. Denying them all the extra-sensory insight and power of today's healing superstars, he reduces them to 'mere' *pray-ers*. Wimberism, therefore, with all its arrogance and presumption, receives a crushing rebuke from *James* 5.*

What about 'imagineering' — the technique of recalling hurtful memories in order that Jesus may be

---

*While ignoring the *James* 5 instructions given by the Holy Spirit, John Wimber gives several steps for healing. The first involves an interview. The second is that of arriving at a diagnosis and seeking a word of knowledge from God as to why the person has the sickness. (It may, he claims, be due to some sin or relationship problem.) If a demon is the cause, Wimber will be told so by God.

The third stage is to select the kind of prayer which is appropriate, and the healer must ask God whether He wants to heal the patient now or later, so that he can pray the correct prayer. Does God want the healer to give a prophecy as to when the sickness will go, or does He want the illness commanded out immediately? Does fantasised into the remembered scene to heal the pain? Is any of this discussed in *James 5*? Of course not, because none of the inspired writers of the New Testament had ever heard of these mind-healing methods. They are modern inventions combining outmoded psychotherapy with Eastern mind-power teaching.

What about the laying on of hands? Canon Glennon tells us — 'I found that I could lay hands on people and pray that they be healed, and they were healed, if not immediately, then in a progressive way.' Selwyn Hughes asserts: 'The laying on of hands is one of God's ordained delivery systems that brings His healing power to men and women.' Certainly the apostles employed the laying on of hands in accordance with Christ's special command to them, but *they actually carried out the healings*. They were the true possessors of a personal healing gift, a gift which was designed to authenticate them as instruments of revelation. But when James lays down the procedure to be followed by ordinary church elders he says nothing whatsoever about laying hands on the sick, because the duty of the elders is to *pray* for healing and not to *effect* it. If we cannot actually *give* healing to people, then we have no business laying hands on them.

It goes without saying that *James 5* excludes such activities as the dispensing or calling down of the Holy

He want the prayer to be in tongues or in ordinary speech? Stage three will ask God to reveal the answers to these questions.

The fourth stage is the so-called 'prayer engagement', in which John Wimber lays hands on the sick, and calls down the Holy Spirit until people shake, sob, scream, collapse, etc.

The question which we must ask is this: By what right or authority does anyone produce an elaborate scheme for Holy Spirit healing which owes nothing to God's revealed procedure, and which completely contradicts God's procedure? Wimber's constant claims to have received his knowledge directly from the Holy Spirit are proved to be utterly spurious.

Spirit, yet this is commonplace in present-day healing ministries. By what power or authority may an elder at a sick-bed give orders to the Holy Spirit? What single text or example do we have in the New Testament to tell us that this is elders' work? The answer is that there is no such text. Equally, *James 5* provides no basis for claims that the Spirit's healing power will come to some people as they are placed in hypnotic trances, while others will experience heat sensations, excitement, electrical ting-lings, tongues-speaking and so on. All these things are widely expected in charismatic healing today, but James knows nothing about them, nor does any other New Testament writer.

It is quite amazing how things can come to be taken for granted in some charismatic circles when there is absolutely no sign of them in the pages of the Bible! Such phenomena are entirely 'extra-biblical', or in plain terms, unbiblical. James, in his God-given procedure for healing prayer, effectively outlaws and condemns all this dominating and manipulating of the Spirit, togeth-er with the desire to feel strange bodily sensations. His method is markedly different in its simplicity, straight-forwardness and humble dependence upon God. The procedure laid down by James is nothing more or less than a ministry of tender care and earnest prayer.

When one considers the vast chasm between the teaching of James and the activities of modern healers it is not surprising that the healing authors have so little time for him. John Wimber can think of no good reason to give even a short chapter to *James 5* in all his 300-page book on healing. Indeed he cannot fill a page on *James 5*, and why should he? James says not one word in support of all the processes which Wimber advocates. Canon Glennon attempts no credible exposi-tion of the *James* passage, taking less than two pages to say that the 'prayer of faith' is the kind of prayer which will claim a guaranteed healing from God. Colin Urquhart is equally superficial in his treatment of *James 5*, also taking a mere two pages to tell us that the oil symbolises the Holy Spirit and stimulates the faith which will infallibly secure healing. He makes no attempt to relate the words of James to the overriding principle of God's Word that all prayer is subject to the will of God.

Needless to say, Agnes Sanford, and those who copy her, have virtually nothing to say on *James 5* at all, and nor do Catholic charismatic healers such as Father Francis MacNutt. One could name names endlessly, for the fact is that James is only ever quoted out of context by this school of authors. He is never taken seriously. Charismatic healers have no hesitation in copying methods from non-evangelical quarters, even from occult sources, but they cannot and will not respect *James 5*, which is God's only model for the ongoing churches of Christ. Anyone who sincerely believes in the absolute authority of God's Word must be deeply concerned and dismayed at the unprecedented departure from the plain rules of that Word on the part of so many people who claim to be evangelical.

Before we present the *positive* application of *James 5*, there is one further feature of charismatic thinking which is confuted in this passage — the oft repeated idea that there is a difference between *afflictions* and *sicknesses*. Most healing writers claim that Christians are meant to suffer *afflictions* (ie: buffetings, disappointments and persecution from their environment), but not *sicknesses*. Having made this distinction they then try to persuade us that all Paul's statements about bearing numerous troubles, weaknesses and infirmities must refer to *external* afflictions and never to personal sickness.

James, however, frustrates any attempt to draw a

distinction between external afflictions and internal illnesses by joining them together and saying that the believer's response to them is *identical*. The response in each case is to pray for help, but to do so with a readiness to accept that God *may* require us to suffer the trial with patience. Here is how James sweeps away this modern charismatic theory. After two strong exhortations to patience he says: *Take, my brethren, the prophets, who have spoken in the name of the Lord, for an example of suffering affliction, and of patience (James 5.10)*. Many of the prophets suffered terrible persecution — an *external* affliction. But James immediately links this form of suffering with that of sickness, thereby telling his readers to be prepared for both forms of trial. He says — *Ye have heard of the patience of Job, and have seen the end of the Lord; that the Lord is very pitiful, and of tender mercy (James 5.11)*.

It is true, of course, that Job suffered other trials besides sickness. He suffered the loss of his family, substance, influence and reputation, as well as the hostile judgement of his friends. Nevertheless, paramount in his sorrows was a terrible, wasting bodily illness, which left him racked with pain day and night, and rendered him vile and pitiful in the estimation of his friends, neighbours and former employees. From James, therefore, we learn that sickness as well as affliction will visit the Lord's people and that our response should be the same in either case. We must pray, but we *may* have to bear the trial with patience and trust.

We learn very clearly from the example of Job that sickness *may* have to be endured for a long season. James will soon be speaking about the possibility of healing blessing in answer to prayer, but first he warns us that an illness may be protracted if God has a purpose in that illness. He speaks of *the end of the Lord*, or *the outcome of the Lord's dealings (NASB).* The *end* of the Lord is from the Greek *telos*, which signifies the result, the outcome or the goal or purpose. James indicates very clearly that God may have a goal to achieve by illness, and if this is the case then we may have to bear it patiently. Needless to say, charismatic healing authors totally ignore these words. As far as they are concerned James never wrote them!

Though James carefully prepares us for the possibility that God will not always remove the illness, today's healers rush straight to the healing promise, interpreting it as though every sick believer is guaranteed a healing. They write as though sickness is always a devilish intrusion which God would never use for any higher purpose. But James unquestionably teaches the opposite. What may the Lord's purpose or goal be in leaving us sick, if only for a time? The range of purposes reflected in many Bible passages is very wide. For the present let us simply note that these purposes range through sanctifying us, training us for future service, imparting to us some additional virtue, weaning us from the world, deepening our relationship with the Lord, and enabling us to give a powerful witness from the context of adversity. The key matter is that there is often an *end* or purpose or goal to be achieved.

No trial, affliction or sickness is to be regarded as an accident or a totally purposeless nuisance. It is right to seek immediate medical help and to pray for healing. It is wrong to lose patience and to throw away the promise — *that all things work together for good to them that love God.* To summarise, we are taught in *James 5* that for both categories of suffering — external troubles and bodily illnesses — the following attitudes should be adopted by believers:

(1) We must expect them both.

(2) We must pray for help and deliverance.

(3) We must be prepared to exercise patience, for God may strengthen us to bear the problem rather than take it away.

(4) We must believe that a problem not removed serves a purpose which will work to our eternal good, and may stand as a witness to others.

The Procedure for Healing

Is any sick among you? let him call for the elders ... and let them pray ... and pray one for another, that ye may be healed (James 5.14-16).

The procedure laid down in *James 5* for ministering to the sick is very precise, and we need to pay close attention to the words which James employs. Exactly who 'qualifies' for the ministry of the elders in the home? First, we are instructed to make a distinction with regard to the *severity* of an illness, for when James says — *Is any sick among you?* — he chooses a word (Gk: *astheneo*) which indicates that the sufferer is strengthless and feeble. This word is normally appropriate to sufferers who are bedridden or helpless. In *John 5*, for example, we read of Bethesda's porches in which *lay a great multitude of impotent folk, of blind, halt, withered* ... (*Astheneo* is here translated *impotent*.)

Alongside this term indicating great weakness we note the fact that the sick person cannot get out to the meetings and must call for the elders. Also, James tells the elders to *pray over* the sick person, which indicates that they are standing over a person who is prostrate. Final proof that the sick person is bedridden is to be seen in the phrase — *and the Lord shall raise him up*. He will be *raised* from the bed of sickness. Naturally we may extend 'bedridden' to include people who are housebound by their ailment.

However, we know even more about the sufferer in

James 5 than the fact that he is bedridden. We know that he has been seriously ill for some time — long enough at least to become very discouraged. This is no temporary backache or bout of 'flu. We know this because James uses another word to describe this person's sickness when he says — *And the prayer of faith shall save the SICK*. Here the word *sick (kamno)* refers to *weariness* or exhaustion, including weariness of mind. (In *Hebrews 12.3* the same word appears — *lest ye be WEARIED and faint in your minds*. In *Revelation 2.3* the same word occurs in the phrase — *and hast not FAINTED*.)

The picture before us, therefore, is of a person who is so sick that he has become despondent and exhausted by the duration and apparent hopelessness of his condition. It is a case of housebound illness which has become a great burden and discouragement, unlike an 'ordinary' affliction which has a predictable duration and is generally susceptible to treatment. In the latter case we have no great cause to be deeply despondent and discouraged. If 'ordinary' illness strikes there is no need for the special bedside service which is reserved for people who are suffering great weariness and despondency either because the illness is so very serious, or because it shows no sign of responding to treatment.

The bedside prayer service is not designed to be used for 'lesser' illnesses, or for our 'walking wounded' (who could include quite advanced cancer patients). If believers can get to the services and prayer meetings they are not housebound, and so the special ministry of elders is inappropriate no matter how serious their illness. Is there no ministry of prayer for milder illnesses and the 'walking wounded'? There most certainly is, but for these cases a second and much simpler procedure is given in *James 5*.

Once James has finished describing the sick-room

procedure, he deals with all other cases of illness in the command — *Pray one for another, that ye may be healed (James 5.16)*. This instruction clearly includes private prayer as well as the earnest pleadings of the church prayer meeting, but there are no special bedside gatherings.

If we feel that the 'walking wounded' are being denied a blessing by this arrangement then we need to stop and ask ourselves why we should think this is so. Are we saying that there is some extra potency or healing power available through the elders ministering at the bedside which cannot be secured by ordinary prayer? If we think that there is some mysterious special blessing in the bedside service, then we have fallen into the trap of thinking like Catholics, or like superstitious cult followers who believe that there is special power or 'magic' in a particular piece of ritual. The bedside service is designed exclusively for housebound believers who are despairing under the burden of a seemingly intractable illness. Because they cannot get out to the services the elders of the church will bring to their bedside the comfort and assurance of care and prayer.

Returning to the procedure for the bedridden person, the elders are to attend as a group, showing that what is required is not a gifted healer but a company of praying voices. The principal activity of the elders is prayer, although it goes without saying that they will extend spiritual comfort and counsel as this is the special work of elders all the time. The Holy Spirit would surely not say that the *elders* should be called if no uniquely eldership role was to be exercised! In this connection James indicates that sickness may sometimes be used by God to bring wayward Christians to review their ways, saying — *If he have committed sins, they shall be forgiven him (James 5.15)*.

There is, however, something else which the elders

must do, and it is this activity which is so greatly misunderstood by charismatics. The elders are to anoint the sick person with oil in the name of the Lord. The question is: What precisely is the purpose or significance of this anointing with oil? The answer lies in the word chosen by James to describe it. First, we need to understand that the original Greek does not say *anointing* but simply 'oiling'. Anointing is an old-fashioned English word which conveys the impression that a religious rite is being performed. Two alternative Greek words are used in the New Testament to describe the process of applying oil to someone. One of these is generally employed where the application of oil is done for a purely physical, secular or medical purpose (Greek: *aleipho*), while the other is used where the application of oil has a sacred, spiritual significance (Gk: *chrio*).

The word chosen by James is the *first* of these two, indicating that the rubbing in of oil carried out by the elders had a physical purpose, and not a religious one. Thus Lenski translates the passage, 'Oiling him with oil in the name of the Lord,' and then adds that the word — 'refers to the *common* use of oil. We do not anoint a piece of machinery, we *oil* it.' Oil, or ointment containing various perfumes or medicaments, was extensively used in those days for freshening up, putting a glow into the complexion, applying perfumes, and for soothing sores, easing pain and treating certain maladies. One or two charismatic writers dogmatically claim that oil never had any medical purpose in Bible times, but they merely show their ignorance of the Bible! The very common use of oils and ointments for medical purposes is seen in several Bible passages.

In *Isaiah 1.6* the prophet describes the nation in terms of a person covered from head to toe in wounds, bruises and putrifying sores, and yet to the astonishment of the prophet, these had not been bound up or *mollified with ointment.* Oil and ointment are usually the same word in Old Testament Hebrew; whether greasy or liquid they were prepared from olive or balsam oil. Isaiah's use of this illustration shows just how common-place the use of medicinal oil was.

Jeremiah also shows how common medicinal oil was, asking, *Is there no balm in Gilead; is there no physician there? (Jeremiah 8.22).* Gilead was famous for its oil of balsam, and Jeremiah's point is that the Israelites had as much access to the Divine Physician as they had to medicinal ointment, yet they sought no treatment for the wounds of sin. In the parable of the good Samaritan the Lord Jesus causes the Samaritan to bind up the wounds of the one who had been robbed and beaten — *pouring in oil and wine.*

To understand the *James 5* passage, we must there-fore remember that oil was a standard medical remedy, and also that James uses the secular or physical verb for 'oiling'. The correct view of the passage is that the application of oil carried out by the elders was an administration of simple medical comfort.*

It is not necessary to think that James advocated the use of oil as a *curative*, but he certainly prescribed it as a means of providing comfort and for the soothing of bed sores and so on. We should not be in the least surprised

*Other texts where this non-religious oiling word is used confirm that James had physical relief in mind. In *Matthew 6.17* Jesus tells the person who fasts to oil his head and wash his face, so that he will look well groomed and fresh, and not at all like someone who is fasting. *Mark 16.1* tells us how the two Marys, with Salome, brought fragrant spices in oil (or ointment) to apply to the body of the Lord. This was the custom of those times, and not a religious act. In *Luke 7.38* we read of the sinful woman who washed the feet of Jesus with her tears and then applied oil, no doubt fragrant oil. *John 12.3* records how Mary of Bethany took a pound of costly ointment and applied it to the feet of the Saviour. In none of these instances did the 'anointing' have any religious significance, and so the non-religious term for oiling is used.

that James commands the elders to place this kind of ordinary, physical help alongside prayer. It is no good being heavenly-minded and of no earthly use, and this is the chief lesson to be derived from the application of oil. Elsewhere James says that if a member of the church is impoverished or hungry and a fellow believer says, 'Go in peace; be warmed and filled,' without giving whatever is needed, then that believer's faith is dead and useless. Similarly, how dare the elders go to the sick-bed and pray for God's healing blessing without attempting to supply the obvious needs of the sufferer.

We remember that there was no welfare provision in those days and many Christians were extremely poor. It is easy to visualise such a person — a stricken bread-winner perhaps — unable to afford a physician and covered in bed sores. We may be sure that when elders gave this basic nursing care they would have done so in a fitting and ethical manner, perhaps using a suitable relative, or taking with them someone like *Phebe our sister, which is a servant of the church*.

The provision of comforting oil would also have served to correct any wrong ideas about divine healing. If the sick person had succumbed to the idea that 'ordinary' care was contrary to divine healing, then the action of the elders would have corrected this mistake. The sufferer would have been shown that proper care is necessary in sickness even for those who are trusting in God for ultimate healing blessing.

In our day we have a 'dynamic equivalent' for the ministry of oil, which is the duty of elders to ensure that sick believers are receiving proper care and attention. Occasionally we find that something has gone wrong, in that an elderly, sick person has somehow missed out on suitable medical care. Elders will also need to look out for other areas of need, and these are sometimes glaringly obvious. What about financial problems, care of children and other pressing worries? The oil of *James 5* is without doubt the 'substance' and example of a ministry of care, and not the inauguration of a religious rite.

Those who feel that James speaks of an anointing which symbolises the presence of God or the receiving of the Spirit should take note of the fact that there are only two symbolic ordinances in the New Testament — baptism and the Lord's Supper. There are no other rites involving sacred symbolism in the Christian faith. Prayer and prayer alone brings the blessing of God to believers who are ill, and the application of oil serves no essential part in the securing of that blessing. What are we saying to God if we feel the need to do something else (that is — some religious ceremony) in addition to praying? Are we telling Him that we cannot trust prayer alone, and we need an outwardly visible sacred rite to give us 'something extra' to depend upon?

Some put their trust in a charismatic wonder-healer, others in the mystical significance of anointing with oil! In this way things which are *done* become a substitute for faith and prayer. Many Christians have become like Naaman of old who wanted Elisha to engage in some splendid piece of healing dramatics. He said — *Behold, I thought, He will surely come out to me, and stand, and call on the name of the Lord his God, and strike his hand over the place, and recover the leper (2 Kings 5.11).*

Some of those who argue that the application of oil is a religious symbol base their view on the fact that the 'anointing' is to be done *in the name of the Lord*. However, this in no way indicates that the oiling is a religious ceremony because we are commanded to do *everything* that we do in the name of the Lord, whether temporal or spiritual activities. In using the phrase — *in the name of the Lord* — James means that the elders are to carry out the benevolent aspect of their work as those who have been sent by God to do this (in obedience to His Word) and not merely as kind-hearted individuals. It is the Lord Who is caring for His sick children through the concern, prayers, fellowship and the personal attention of the elders, and the Lord must get the credit and the gratitude of the sufferer. Elders, therefore, are not to put themselves across as wonderful, benevolent people, but they are to take the part of servants of the Lord, representing Him. It is God Who has determined that His beloved people shall be sympathised with and prayed for. The elders give practical help (the oiling) in the name of the Lord to show that *He* cares for the sufferer.

What Is the Prayer of Faith?

When James says that the prayer of faith shall save the sick, does he mean that healing is *bound* to result, as long as the right quality of faith is present? This, of course, is the view of most charismatic healing writers. They think that healing will definitely follow when both the healer and the sick person possess absolute certainty that the illness will be cured. So confident of this are the more exhibitionist healers that they have made the prayer of faith the executive instrument of healing! Often their prayer of faith is no more than a command to the illness to depart!

The assumption that healing is guaranteed rests entirely on the terseness of James' language — *the prayer of faith shall save the sick*. Because he adds no qualifying statement such as, 'If it be God's will,' charismatics run away with the idea that it is *always* God's will to heal. However, James takes it for granted that his readers will add this qualifying statement for themselves, because it is an overriding principle of the Bible that *all* prayer is subject to the sovereign will and wisdom of the Lord. James has just insisted on this in the previous chapter, where he condemns believers who plan their affairs without due submission to God's superintending will. He provides a great motto text which must never be laid aside — *Ye ought to say, If the Lord will, we shall live, and do this, or that* (*James 4.15*).

If charismatic authors would only read a few verses either side of the passages which they bend to fit their theories they would get some big surprises. Is the prayer for healing exempt from the rule that all prayer is subject to God's will? Listen to James again — *If the Lord will, we shall live!* This principle applies to all our prayers no matter what the subject, and must always be assumed to apply by the Lord's people. In *1 John 5.14* we read: *If we ask any thing ACCORDING TO HIS WILL, he heareth us.* Once again we remember that James calls attention to Job, exhorting us to be willing to suffer with patience, should this be the purpose of the Lord for us. The idea that healing is guaranteed so long as the right quality of faith is present arises from a highly superficial reading of the passage.

But why did James express himself in such an unguarded way? Was it not predictable that someone might forget about the sovereign will of God and consequently misunderstand his words? The answer to this is that James' sentence was only intended to prevent people from attaching too much importance to the 'anointing' with oil. Just in case people might think that the oil played some part in getting a blessing, James added the corrective words — *the prayer of faith shall save the sick*. We may amplify his words as follows: 'Apply oil in the name of the Lord, but remember that faithful prayer is the only means by which God's healing blessing may be secured.'

The fact that healing is not guaranteed is surely

proved from Paul's experience, recorded in *2 Corinthians 12.7-10*. Here Paul speaks of the thorn in his flesh, which was without doubt a bodily illness, notwithstanding the attempts made by charismatic writers to prove that it was his earthly enemies! Paul's personal experience proves conclusively that it is not always God's will to remove sickness. Three times he pleaded with God for its removal, and then God indicated to him that the illness must be borne in the strength which He would give. (The proof that Paul's thorn was a physical affliction is provided as an appendix to this chapter.)

Returning to the *James 5* passage, we note that James is careful to leave God's sovereignty in place when he says — *The effectual fervent prayer of a righteous man availeth much (James 5.16)*. The word translated *prayer* in this text is the humblest Greek word for prayer, coming from the verb 'to beg'. It means to plead, request, ask, and to petition. It is not a demanding, claiming, insisting kind of word, but one which recognises, and is ready to bow to, the higher wisdom and authority of Almighty God. It is a pleading word; the prayer of one who hopes to prevail upon the Lord, but who recognises that He may have a higher plan. The kind of pleading prayer which James has in mind cannot be offered by someone who has made up his or her mind how God must answer! It is not the prayer of someone determined to get his own way, come what may. It is not a form of will-power which attempts to bend circumstances to our own will.

We are to make humble petitions based on wonderful grounds: first, that our God has the power to do anything He chooses, and secondly, that He invites us to *ask* Him for healing. Nevertheless we do not insist on healing as a right, but in all our asking we are ready to trust the perfect plan of our heavenly Father. The prayer of faith is therefore not the prayer of people who have convinced themselves that the healing is already accomplished. Such an attitude is mind-power, not prayer! The prayer of faith is a prayer offered by those who recognise that God is supreme and perfect, and that He will bring things to pass according to His perfect will and timing. The true prayer of faith *never* takes God's sovereignty away from Him.

In the final part of his instructions about praying for the sick, James emphasises that God invites petitions from those who live godly lives. While everything is subject to His supreme wisdom, yet prayer definitely avails to secure a healing response, and we may therefore expect to experience His blessing frequently. James assures us that — *The effectual fervent prayer of a righteous man availeth much*. The word translated *effectual* comes from the Greek for energy, activity or work. The meaning of the phrase is that when we strive to live lives which are obedient and pleasing to the Lord, then our prayers have a persuasive energy before Him, and therefore will accomplish much.

Sadly, the enormous incentive to pray which this promise should give us is often lost because we have a mistaken view of God's predestinating purpose. Many Christians manifest a deadly form of fatalism in their prayers, sounding as though they do not really think it is worth praying at all. Their prayers lack any note of conviction, urgency, pleading or persuasion. Whatever they ask for, they think that God will do whatever He already intended before they started praying. Prayer, in other words, makes no difference, and so they conclude every prayer with the hopeless lamentation — 'According to Thy will'. They utter these words as though the whole exercise of prayer is a pointless formality.

But James assures us that the prayers of God's children possess persuasive energy, and therefore we must not pray as though God has made up His mind irrespective of what we may ask. We are meant to pray as those who have been invited by God to bring appeals and petitions before Him. He has repeatedly promised to listen and to respond, always, of course, applying His supreme wisdom and plans to the case, and it is this that we should have in mind when we say, 'According to Thy will.' We should not have in mind the idea that God will ignore our appeals unless they just happen to coincide with His predetermined plan.

We must make our appeals on the ground that God has promised to take the *fullest* account of them. He is ready to be moved and persuaded by our cries, unless in a given case He has something better in mind, or some higher purpose to achieve through the illness. Many times we shall prove the truth of the words — *the prayer of faith shall save the sick*. If we believe in the sovereignty of God we may not understand this and we may wonder how it is possible for the God Who predetermines all things to be prevailed upon to change His will on anything. How can our prayers make any difference? This is the thought which lies behind the fatalistic style of prayer.

We offer two explanations which are frequently advanced to solve this riddle, though we must acknowledge that God's readiness to 'change' the order of events at our request is a great mystery. One explanation is that God often brings His intended purposes to pass by first moving in the hearts of His children to pray for them. Thus He is sovereign in all things, yet we are instrumental in securing His glorious blessing. The other explanation is that God really does clothe His people with the high privilege of responsible and voluntary intercession, so that blessings will be secured when they pray, and missed when they do not. How, then, is God still sovereign? The answer, according to this explanation, is that God took account of all our prayers before time began, and predetermined that they should be answered in the fulness of time.*

When we pray for those who are ill, we must do so with a true conviction that our heavenly Father is ready to listen and to change matters. We must never say, 'According to Thy will,' in a spirit of *fatalistic resignation*, but rather in a spirit of readiness to accept that God may have a purpose in someone's sickness. Therefore, if our prayers for healing are not answered, we shall continue to trust Him as our heavenly Father Who possesses infinite love, goodness, wisdom and power, and Who has a sovereign plan for all His people.

What Exactly Should We Pray For?

Another remarkable encouragement to prayer is provided in *James 5* with the example of Elijah and the rains (*James 5.17-18*). Elijah was inspired by God to cry out in the presence of King Ahab for the cessation of dew and rain, and consequently the rains failed for three and a half years. Elijah looked for the direct intervention of the Lord in the matter, an expectation which is commended to us as we pray for sick believers. The application for us is this: God is prepared to overrule natural processes of disease and sickness by *direct intervention*, if necessary, in answer to prayer. Therefore, we may pray uninhibitedly for the recovery of sick believers without feeling that the Lord limits Himself to the use of ordinary means such as surgery or medication.

Sometimes we hear friends praying for those who are ill as though God strictly confines Himself to guiding the physicians in their diagnosis and treatment, or

*This reasoning should not be applied to prayer for salvation, for God's predestinating love in salvation is clearly described as being unconditional.

guiding the hands of surgeons as they operate. These friends seem reluctant to believe that the Lord will ever go beyond these normal agencies of recovery to place His own healing touch upon the sick person. It should be obvious to us that the Lord does deal directly with the sick, if only from the fact that medical science was hopelessly inadequate for most serious diseases in New Testament times. Therefore when James said of the sick person — *the Lord shall raise him up* — he referred to the direct healing touch of the Lord.

It is right, of course, to pray for the guidance of God for doctors and nurses, but it is not right to *limit* God's healing method to rational means. We live in privileged days, when by God's common grace the advance of learning has produced remedies for so many illnesses. We realise also that it is a general principle of the Bible that God does not use *miraculous* means where He has given *ordinary* means. However, where conditions are not safely and certainly treatable by medical science, the Lord may well choose to move in a direct manner to heal and restore. If a believer recovers from a form of cancer which *sometimes* responds to treatment, that person will never know for certain whether God healed the condition *directly*, or whether He blessed the treatment, but it matters little because the healed believer will give thanks and glory to God either way.

The point is that we should pray for the sick, believing that God is not limited by the skill of medical science. How often we see believers recovering unusually quickly from hospitalisation because the Lord not only safely superintended the work of the surgeon, but also granted a direct blessing for speedy recovery. Of course we can only speak in general terms because we have no way of investigating or assessing the wonderful works of God, but at least we must be careful not to limit our expectation of what He may do.

In the light of all this it should be clear to us that God's healing blessings are not usually suitable to be paraded about before unbelievers as startling proof of the existence and the power of God. By the nature of the case we cannot usually be sure whether God healed by medication or in a direct way. Perhaps an isolated missionary, far from the nearest doctor or clinic, can be more certain when the Lord gives a most remarkable recovery, but more often than not we cannot determine the manner of God's working. These blessings are not intended to provide miraculous proofs to a cynical world, but as believers *we* shall praise God for the many, many times He has blessed and restored us; often in small illnesses, sometimes in major ones.

Does the Lord place any limit on the *kind* of healings He will bring about in the lives of His people? While we must not restrict Him to working within the limits of achievement attainable by medical skill, does this mean that we may look to Him for the same kind of healings as those performed by the Lord Jesus Christ on earth — *The blind receive their sight, and the lame walk . . . the deaf hear, the dead are raised up . . .* ? In other words — how great is our scope when it comes to praying for those who are sick? The answer suggested by the terms which James employs is that healing will generally be associated with weakening, debilitating illnesses rather than with *fixed conditions* (such as blindness or limblessness) which may be suffered by people who are otherwise in very good health.

Remember that James uses terms which indicate conditions of weakness and feebleness together with weariness or mental despondency. The sick person who calls for the elders needs to be raised from a sickbed, and so the illness which is in mind seems to be an active and worsening disease of some kind. The healing of settled physical handicaps was certainly included in the wonderful sign-miracles of the Lord and of His apostles, but afflictions of this kind do not, on the face of it, appear to be in mind in *James 5*. Nothing is impossible with God Who can do whatever He chooses, but we are not given a warrant by James to bring every kind of disability before the Lord in prayer.

Approaching the matter from another direction, we refer again to the 'motto text' of *James 4.15 — Ye ought to say, If the Lord will, we shall live, and do this, or that*. If we have prayed for the recovery of a person for some while and find that our prayer is unavailing, then it may be time to recognise that God in His sovereignty has called the sufferer to bear with that affliction. Perhaps we should shift the main object of our praying to seeking strength and comfort for that person. This would be in line with *2 Corinthians 12*, where Paul was shown that his infirmity would not be removed by prayer, but that he should draw all the relief and strength he needed from the Lord. *James 5* does not give us a *carte blanche* commission to claim everything from the Lord, and it is necessary for us to bow to His supreme will when persistent prayer for healing meets with no healing response, and to adjust the aim of our petitions accordingly.

Take the problem of handicaps in children, brought about by genetic irregularities or brain injury at birth. Naturally there will be much earnest prayer for these infants. But what if some form of ailment or handicap very evidently becomes the fixed condition of a child even after much prayer has been offered? At this point we should perhaps shift the focus of our prayer so that we pray for the child's safety from all the secondary hazards (such as infections) to which such children are vulnerable, remembering that we may, as a church fellowship, need to bear them up in prayer throughout life's journey.

Paul's Thorn in the Flesh

There can be no doubt that Paul's thorn in the flesh was a physical illness. Modern attempts by charismatic teachers to interpret the thorn as symbolising a personal enemy or enemies must be dismissed as far-fetched exegetical gymnastics. These teachers are desperately anxious to prove that no Christian should suffer sickness because (they say) God has promised healing to all. Paul's illness is an obvious embarrassment to this theory and it must therefore be explained away.

Charismatics claim that Paul's thorn must refer to his persecutors because this figure of speech is used in the Old Testament to describe human enemies. The Canaanites were *thorns in the sides* of the Israelites. However, it does not follow that *thorns* will always stand for the same kind of trouble throughout the Bible. When Paul refers to his trouble he speaks of a *singular* thorn, and he specifically says that it was *in the flesh*.

Unanswerable proof of the fact that Paul's thorn was *not* his enemies is to be found in his response to the Lord's command. God told him that this thorn would not be taken away in answer to prayer. In other words, Paul must no longer pray for its removal, nor must he encourage others to do so. But Paul repeatedly urges the churches to join him in prayer for deliverance from his *enemies*, and utters wonderful words of testimony to the effect that he has been delivered from them. The proof passages are these:

Now I beseech you . . . that ye strive together with me in your prayers to God for me; that I may be delivered from them that do not believe in Judaea . . . (Romans 15.30-31).

Finally, brethren, pray for us . . . that we may be delivered from unreasonable and wicked men (2 Thessalonians 3.1-2).

But thou hast fully known my . . . persecutions . . . at Antioch, at Iconium, at Lystra; what persecutions I endured: but out of them all the Lord delivered me (2 Timothy 3.10-11).

At my first answer no man stood with me, but all men forsook me: I pray God that it may not be laid to their charge. Notwithstanding the Lord stood with me, and strengthened me; that by me the preaching might be fully known, and that all the Gentiles might hear: and I was delivered out of the mouth of the lion. And the Lord shall deliver me from every evil work, and will preserve me unto his heavenly kingdom: to whom be glory for ever and ever. Amen (2 Timothy 4.16-18).

Because Paul prayed uninhibitedly for deliverance from his persecutors, and testified to God's answers to those prayers, we may be sure that his thorn in the flesh (which God would not remove) was a bodily illness of some kind. There is one text which confirms very definitely that Paul suffered with his health. In *Galatians*

4.13-14 he writes: *But you know that it was because of a bodily illness that I preached the gospel to you the first time; and that which was a trial to you in my bodily condition you did not despise or loathe, but you received me as an angel of God, as Christ Jesus Himself (NASB).*

In the light of all this we see no justification for altering the usual meaning attached to *infirmities* in *2 Corinthians 12.9*. *Infirmities* (Greek: *strengthlessness*) here refers to weakness due to some bodily illness or disability. Paul tells us of how the Lord said to him: *My grace is sufficient for thee: for my strength is made perfect in weakness. Most gladly therefore will I rather glory in my infirmities, that the power of Christ may rest upon me.*

9
Imagineering
The new wave of mind and memory healing

IN THE NEW SPATE of healing books numerous charismatic authors have leapt on to the 'Yonggi Cho' bandwagon of visualising prayer results into existence. One writer, David A. Seamands, for example, writes in his book *Healing of Memories*, 'Faith has been called a form of sanctified imagination. This means we pray using our imagination to visualise people as healed and freed from the painful chains of their past; that we picture them as changed and made new.'

Authors like Seamands are committed to the idea once loved by secular psychiatrists that buried or suppressed hurts will cripple people unless they are brought to the surface one by one, exposed to view, and purged away. Seamands and others go so far as to say that *not even God* can heal damaged emotions and memories unless this routine is carried out and the sufferer brought 'face to face' with the diseased memory. The method is 'Christianised' by means of introducing the risen Lord, by the imagination, into the sufferer's past affairs.

First the sick or depressed person is invited to recall

times of emotional distress in childhood. Then, by use of the imagination, the sufferer must re-create the scene and enter into it once again, seeing it through the eyes of a child. Once carried away in the spirit of fantasy, the 'child' is then urged to imagine Jesus in the incident. The Saviour may fit whatever mental image the sufferer wants, but He is to be imagined in realistic detail, speaking words of comfort and assurance. Then the patient (as a child) must speak words of forgiveness to the parents, or whoever was the cause of the childhood hurt, and so purge away the repressed cause of all their problems.

Patients, or 'counsellees' as they are sometimes called, often get completely carried away as they imagine remarkable scenes, hearing their imagined characters saying extraordinary things. Roman Catholic charismatic memory-healers (who are widely accepted and approved by evangelical charismatics) employ the same techniques but generally substitute Mary for Jesus as the healing, consoling figure which the 'child' meets in the fantasy. The enormous sales figures achieved by books advocating these mind-healing techniques should be a cause of grave concern to orthodox Bible Christians because fantasising is a self-induced delusion which shatters the scriptural rule that the rational mind must be in constant control of our thinking.

The visualising of Christ is clearly a serious breach of the second commandment because it involves conjuring up a detailed mental image of the risen, glorified Lord. The commandment says — *Thou shalt not make unto thee any graven image, or any likeness of any thing that is in heaven above, or that is in the earth beneath . . . Thou shalt not bow down thyself to them, nor serve them.* We may not reproduce or depict in wood, stone, or by mental fantasy, the glorious and infinite God, with a view to substituting this for the spiritual reality. It is wrong and sinful to manufacture our own visualised Christ, and to make Him say words which we want Him to say, to cuddle and caress us, and so forth. Those who teach people to do these things against the expressly revealed will of God are guilty of great profanity and indifference to the Lord's authority.

We have a Saviour Who, in a very shadowy form, we may certainly visualise. It is no sin to have a *general* sense of the Lord's human form. Indeed, the fact that the Saviour clothed Himself with human flesh, and took back to Heaven a glorified body, is an encouragement and help to us as we approach Him. But to clothe that shadowy concept with hazel eyes, brown hair, light or dark skin, particular articles of clothing, or a specific facial expression according to our tastes and desires is to press far beyond a legitimate awareness of His glorified humanity, into the domain of fiction and fantasy.

We are to worship *in spirit and in truth*. How can a mental picture be true if we have invented it? How do we know what the Saviour looks like? How do we know what expression He wears? Perhaps we have sinned and our Saviour is frowning at us, not smiling. It is highly significant that the people counselled by charismatic memory-healers all encounter a smiling Saviour who never frowns, reproves, chastises, warns or commands. They invent for themselves a Saviour Who will comfort and console them, flatter and serve them, rather than bow before the Saviour revealed in the Bible.

The risen Lord showed Himself to Paul to qualify him as an apostle — one who had seen the Lord. But Paul tells us that he was the very last person to see the risen Lord (before He shall come again). Paul was one *born out of due time*, as the last of the apostles. For the rest of us the rule is that the Lord is to be approached exclusively *by faith*, and worshipped *in spirit*. We are to know Christ as He is presented in the Scriptures, and we must never add to that revelation or take anything from it. We are to know Christ by the qualities and character revealed in the Bible, not by imagining Him.

We are to know Christ by the plans and purposes which He reveals in His Word, and we are to love Him on account of His wonderful promises. Paul prays for the Ephesians, that — *Christ may dwell in your hearts by faith.* This is the way to grasp the breadth and length and depth and height, and to know the love of Christ which passes knowledge. It is *not* the Christian faith to turn from the Word as the source of all knowledge of God, and to seek to know Christ and His power by 'imagineering' (as the new jargon puts it). An invented Christ speaking invented words is a false Christ; a manufactured Christ; a make-believe Christ, and even worse — a stage-managed Christ. He is an illusion, springing from wilful disobedience to the Word and a blasphemous readiness to subordinate Almighty God to human control.

In view of the seriousness of the error in this teaching and its soaring popularity, this chapter will review more closely what some of the popular mind-healing writers are saying and doing. Rita Bennett represents this school of thought. Famous in charismatic circles through her co-authorship with her husband Dennis Bennett of *The Holy Spirit and You*, she issued in 1982 a book entitled *Emotionally Free*, which has already been reprinted many times.

Rita Bennett began 'inner healing' (or healing by fantasising) in 1977, her first patient being a middle-aged woman said to be on the verge of a nervous breakdown. This lady is given the name 'Meg' in the book. Having discovered that Meg had suffered an unhappy childhood, Mrs Bennett asked her to focus on a memory of a particular childhood 'hurt'. At the age of three Meg had felt ignored and rejected when her parents were engaged in a furious argument. Mrs Bennett urged her to visualise Jesus in the scene, and to imagine Him just as she would like Him to be. After a few minutes Meg announced that she could see Jesus vividly. She was a child, and Jesus was stooping to pick her up in His arms, saying, 'I won't leave you. I will never forsake you.'

Her imaginary experience moved her to tears and she exclaimed that she now felt so much better — 'so protected'. Rita Bennett recalls that she 'waited to let her bask in the comfort of Jesus' love.' Then she urged Meg to re-enter her fantasy as a three-year-old in order to tell her parents that she would forgive them for their rejection of her.

Mrs Bennett recounts a similar case involving a young man named Jim, who suffered from insecurity, frustration, anger and rejection. Under the 'guidance of the Holy Spirit' Jim remembered the rejection he felt as a schoolboy. Being dyslexic, he 'blanked out' one day during a test, and cried, with the result that his teacher exposed him to ridicule. Rita Bennett seized on this memory and asked Jim to visualise the scene, which he did, including Jesus in his mental picture. Soon Jim's voice became rather excited and he exclaimed, 'He's kneeling down beside me!'

'What's He saying to you?' asked Mrs Bennett.

'He says His love for me will help me learn and help me accept myself. He says He'll make me able to forgive my teacher too.'

Continuing in his 'visualising' mode, Jim spoke to his teacher, expressing his forgiveness, and thus he 'set himself free' from the binding power of his suppressed inner hostility.

Rita Bennett maintains that even Christians who have sincerely tried to live for God may get stuck and find it impossible to pray at all because of a 'hidden agenda' inside them. This may consist of past hurts or problems which have been locked away in the depth of the soul — 'so that even the Holy Spirit cannot touch them'. She insists that God cannot help or heal until the 'sufferer' brings these things to the surface, remembers them, and then 'releases' them to God in a visualising session.

Where does Mrs Bennett find a word of all this in the Bible? The answer is, nowhere! She beats about the bush with elaborate pseudo-scientific explanations. The nearest we get to a theological explanation is a quotation of an astonishing sentiment from Watchman Nee, who said that neither God nor the devil could do anything in our lives without first obtaining our consent. Mrs Bennett extends this idea to the point where God cannot heal our emotional infirmities until we have located the cause and voluntarily relinquished any suppressed bad attitudes.

The question of whether these things are taught in the Bible is dismissed on the feeble grounds that while Jesus was physically present He did not need to be visualised into a sufferer's situation. This hardly accounts for the silence of all the New Testament books from *Acts* to *Revelation* which recorded the formative years of the church (and ministered to it) *after* the ascension of the Lord.

In one 'healing' carried out through the counselling of Rita Bennett, the sufferer was antagonistic to Christ and was not prepared for the name of Jesus to be mentioned. Mrs Bennett agreed instead to talk about 'that Man'. Once again, the sufferer's problem was supposedly rooted in an event which occurred when she was three years old, and she was duly asked to visualise 'that Man' as being with her. Soon she was saying, 'Okay, yes, I see Him. He has on a robe that's woven of natural fibres, and oh! — He knelt down right there on

the sidewalk and looked straight into my eyes and said
— "You're *not* bad!" He put His arm round me and I
felt such love and acceptance!'

As the result of this imaginary meeting with Christ —
including a 'message' from Him which was the very
opposite of what Christ says in the Bible — this hostile
patient supposedly became a Christian. According to
Rita Bennett, it is this kind of detailed manifestation of
Himself to the imagination that Jesus had in mind when
He said — *He that hath my commandments, and keepeth
them . . . I will love him, and will manifest myself to him
(John 14.21).* With typically superficial use of the Bible
she fails to notice that in this text the Lord is talking
about how *He reveals Himself*, not about how others
may order Him up at whim (and to suit their taste) in
their imagination.

The fantasising method led Rita Bennett to heal
someone's fear of horse-riding by making her visualise
the childhood day she fell off a horse. 'We wanted her to
let Jesus come into the scene that had caused her to be
afraid of horses. We joined hands . . . Susie recalled the
experience and said, "Yes, I see Jesus . . . When I fell off
the horse, He put me back on, and now He's walking
along beside me. Jesus looks happy." We then prayed
and ordered any destructive powers affecting her life to
leave.'

We learn from this author that Jesus must be allowed
to heal pre-memory experiences, that is, hurtful
experiences which occurred too early in life to be
remembered. For this we may even have to visualise
right back into our mother's womb! It could be that we
suffer from serious problems because we were not
caressed and cuddled enough in the few minutes after
birth! This experience of deprivation will need to be
imagined so that we can see Jesus in the situation and
speak words of forgiveness to our parents. We may have

to ask God to help us visualise how our parents looked and behaved before we were born. If we cannot accept them *now*, Mrs Bennett tells us, we may be able to accept them *as they were* earlier on!

Any Scripture texts offered by Mrs Bennett to justify all this dangerous nonsense only serve to demonstrate how little respect such charismatic healing authors have for the plain meaning of Bible verses. Here are some examples of texts which are supposed to support the visualising of oneself as a baby in the womb. Mrs Bennett is very pleased with these texts. 'As I searched the Bible,' she says, 'I was delighted to find so many scriptures on prenatal times and birth. God obviously wants us to know what He thinks about it.'

Psalm 22.9 — But thou art he that took me out of the womb: thou didst make me hope when I was upon my mother's breasts.

Isaiah 49.1 — Listen, O isles, unto me; and hearken, ye people, from far; The Lord hath called me from the womb; from the bowels of my mother hath he made mention of my name.

Ephesians 1.4 — According as he hath chosen us in him before the foundation of the world, that we should be holy and without blame before him in love.

John 10.3 — To him the porter openeth; and the sheep hear his voice: and he calleth his own sheep by name, and leadeth them out.

Any reader can judge that these verses give no support whatsoever to the ideas expressed in books like this. But their use is altogether typical of how Scripture is constantly wrested and misused in this new generation of healing books.

Mrs Bennett, like other exponents of 'imagineering' methods, seems to believe that most emotional problems are caused by hurts which others have inflicted. The problem *never* seems to be personal sin such as pride, greed, possessiveness, selfishness and self-centredness. The only sins which her patients ever commit are sins against themselves (like being unforgiving and over-harsh with themselves), and the failure to forgive the other person. As a rule, no other confession of sin is called for; an indication of this writer's non-evangelical view of the human condition.

Rita Bennett is, of course, not original in her mind and memory healing techniques. The present advocates of these ideas lean very heavily on the late Agnes Sanford, a well-known healer whose books have sold in extraordinary numbers since the late 1940s. Mrs Sanford, the wife of an American Episcopal clergyman, was certainly not evangelical in her theology. Her books teem with sentiments which are sometimes mystical, sometimes Catholic, sometimes animistic, sometimes Freudian, but only occasionally are they even vaguely evangelical.

Mrs Sanford had great skill with her pen and a most charming way of relating healing anecdotes. One can easily see how large numbers of people have found her books enchanting reading. However, the reasoning advanced in these books is *never* derived from the Bible, but flows straight out of Mrs Sanford's fertile imagination. Here is a sample of what Bennett, Seamands and so many others copy from this doyenne of modern healers. Agnes Sanford tells the story of a man whose elder brothers had left home as volunteers to fight in the war while he was still a child. He was sure that they would not return and that his heart would break with loneliness. In the event they did return, and happy home life resumed, but the growing young man remained depressed and insecure because his memories remained unhealed.

Mrs Sanford taught this depressed man to visualise that past experience and to project Jesus into the scene.

Soon he could see himself as a boy, leaning sadly on the gate outside his home, a blue cap on his head, with Jesus beside him. Once he saw Jesus in that situation a 'miracle' occurred. The aura of desperation around his memory fled, and he was released from his woes.

Mrs Sanford openly states that her method for healing memories is the same kind of thing which is achieved by 'depth psychology', but whereas the latter causes patients to re-live the past over a period of months, often with much pain and tears, her technique of visualising is comparatively brief, and the pain only fleeting.

Agnes Sanford claimed that a deep knowledge of suffering people was given to her by the Holy Spirit along with healing *and creative* power. She said that by the use of her imagination she found she could 'remote control' the behaviour of her children when they were young, willing away tantrums, and so on. She explained that her healing powers were an extension of this.

Once when she was on a train a rock was hurled through the window badly gashing the forehead of a young man sitting opposite and knocking him unconscious to the floor. Blood spurted so freely that it ran down the aisle, to the consternation of everyone. In the ensuing commotion the train was stopped and the guard telephoned from the trackside for an ambulance. Mrs Sanford tells how she began to pray, strenuously visualising a healed forehead: 'I lent to the prayer the power of my imagination, seeing the wound healed.' In less than ten minutes the man recovered, and within the hour the once gaping wound had become a thin white line like a three-week-old scar. Agnes Sanford holds this up as an example of the use of the *creative* gift possessed by man, a gift which is apparently exercised by force of the imagination, helped by the Holy Spirit.

However, this creative gift which enables us to

visualise healing is utterly contrary to what the Bible tells us about prayer, namely that prayer is *complete* dependence on the power of God to answer, coupled with a readiness to accept His supreme will and purpose in the matter. Prayer is not the art of manipulating the outcome of events by will-power or imagination. Nor is it a kind of mental theatre in which we visualise the Saviour and move Him about the scene like a puppet on strings.

A further insight into the strange ideas of Agnes Sanford (particularly her use of Scripture) is seen in her application of Paul's exhortation — *Walk as children of light*. Mrs Sanford tells us that we must live as people who are charged with living, moving energy like light, which 'vibrates at too high an intensity and too fine a wavelength for the human eye to see'.

Through prayer we can excite this energy into a creative force, and this is what is often sensed as heat or vibrations when the healer lays hands on a suffering person. Mrs Sanford hints that science may one day discover this vibration which Christians can utilise even now. According to her, it is *our* creative force; the use of it is referred to by Paul as walking in the light; and it is nothing less than the spiritual force which God breathed into man at his creation. We include this information here because it serves to show the cult-like mishmash of ideas which gave birth to the mind (and memory) healing techniques which are now enthusiastically embraced by so many charismatic healing writers.

David A. Seamands, a former Methodist missionary, has already been noted as another widely-read author advocating these techniques. He has issued two best-selling books — *Healing for Damaged Emotions* and *Healing of Memories*. Mr Seamands rehearses the familiar ideas — we suffer from emotional sicknesses which God cannot heal until we have discovered the buried memories which cause them. Healing counsellors must pray for guidance that sufferers will recall the offending events, then fill in the scene by the use of their imagination — *visualisation*.

Like Mrs Bennett, Seamands builds his ideas on a foundation of anecdotes and interesting tales about the faculty of memory, rather than deriving them from Scripture. Of course, David Seamands *claims* that his methods are biblical. In a chapter entitled — *Biblical Foundations for Memory Healing* (in *Healing of Memories*) Seamands declares that it is of the utmost importance to understand that these methods have a 'solid foundation' in the Scripture. Yet he immediately launches into a heated criticism of people who reject his methods because they are not described in the Bible. He says, 'If we applied that reasoning to everything, we could be led to fanatical and even dangerous extremes — not wearing clothes with buttons; not driving cars; not using pianos . . . refusing penicillin for a sick child . . .'

In other words, Mr Seamands says we must not prohibit things simply because they are not in the Bible, and this includes his own strange healing techniques. Of course, cars, pianos and penicillin were unknown in Bible times, though other means of transport, musical instruments and medicines were known, and all these are approved in general terms in the biblical narratives. However, the methods of healing advocated by Seamands and others are not the products of modern technology. If they were legitimate, without doubt they would have been advocated in the Bible.

In the event, the entire chapter on *Biblical Foundations* manages to raise no more than four Scripture passages, none of which even remotely justifies these techniques. One of these is *1 Corinthians 13.11*, where Paul speaks of putting away childish things. This text is promptly wrenched from its context and made to say that Paul felt a need to be freed from childish memories which had held him in bondage! The use of such a passage to justify visualising and fantasising is not merely absurd, it is to be condemned as wilful spiritual and intellectual dishonesty.

Another of Seamand's texts is *Hebrews 13.8*, which reads — *Jesus Christ the same yesterday, and to day, and for ever*. Seamands argues that because Jesus is the Lord of time, He will happily enter into our visualising games and thereby heal our past hurts. It should be clear to all unprejudiced readers that this text in no way describes or justifies visualising or fantasising Jesus into existence, and anyone who uses such a text to justify these techniques can hardly be recognised as a person who takes seriously the message of Scripture.

Seamands actually draws his patients further into their problems in his diagnostic procedure, encouraging them to become increasingly preoccupied with their own phobias and problems by prescribing books which drown them in case histories of people with similar problems. He provides recommendations to help anyone who wants to wallow in autobiographies of remorse, shame, guilt, problems of low self-esteem, depression and so on. If broken homes, homosexuality or marital rejection make more appropriate reading, he has plenty of alternative suggestions.

By such prescribed reading people are brought into a self-conscious, introspective, self-pitying state. Now it is hoped that they will be more susceptible to probing questions from the counsellor, as he delves into the memory to drag out every likely piece of deviant behaviour or bitterness which he imagines may be influencing them today. Seamands claims that as he seeks to find a patient's repressed memories, the Holy Spirit prompts him, putting into *his* mind the troubles which the suffering person has forgotten, helping him to fish and trawl for more problems. Unless all these 'hurts' are dredged up and brought to the surface, there can be no healing.

Undaunted by the emotional rape which his shameless intrusion into the deep recesses of the soul may involve, Seamands tries to 'tap' submerged feelings, or 'negative emotions'. As he asks questions he scrutinises patients for what he calls the 'body language' of important emotions — tears, sighs, heavy swallowing, blushes, blotches and nervous laughter.

Once the offending hurtful incidents and memories have been identified, then the counsellees must be taken on the visualising trip into the past, re-living offending events through the eyes of childhood, fantasising Jesus into the situation, and so on. The sufferers are encouraged to pray as little children. Seamands leads the way in a prayer session, saying, 'Now, Lord Jesus, I want to bring before you a little boy/girl. He/she wants to talk to you about some things which have caused a lot of pain.' Seamands tells us that counsellees are often so overcome by the experience that their voices — 'become like those of children'. Adults may cry out, 'Daddy, please don't leave me.'

The simplest comment which can be made on these ideas is that they owe nothing to the Word of God. Indeed, they make the apostle Paul look hopelessly ignorant as an under-shepherd of souls, because he offers none of the techniques so elaborately described by Seamands and others. Imagineering not only violates the second commandment, but it strips God of His power to heal emotional hurts without the assistance of intensive psychological surgery carried out by a trained counsellor. Imagineering also hands out forgiveness and assurance like candy-floss, irrespective of what the Lord God may think.

Only the Son of Man had power on earth to forgive sins, but the central feature of these techniques is the pretence that Jesus was there in the hurtful circumstances of the sufferers even though they never knew it, that He was always on their side, and that they have nothing at all to worry about because He will heal all their wounds and give them happy and successful lives. As anyone who loves evangelical doctrine can see, all this is blatantly anti-Gospel.

Seamands goes so far as to say that counsellors may dispense forgiveness like priests. He says: 'We Protestants have reacted against the Roman Catholic misuse of the confessional and the granting of absolution by priests. In doing so we have given up one of the greatest privileges of our priesthood — being temporary assistants to the Spirit as His instruments to bring forgiveness.' Seamands claims that *Matthew 18.18-20* gives authority for this (a clear indication of his lack of genuine evangelical convictions) and tells us that he keeps handy consecrated communion elements for the purpose of bestowing forgiveness.

Yet despite the compounded layers of anti-biblical error in David Seamands' notions, vast numbers of his books have been printed by a reputable evangelical publishing house, and these penetrate churches everywhere, enjoying a particularly enthusiastic reception in student circles. We urgently need to warn against the shamelessly unbiblical nature of this kind of interference with those in need. It is insulting to God in taking away His power to bless emotionally hurt people simply in response to repentance and prayer; it is blasphemous in its visualisation and manipulation of the Son of God; it is dangerous in the way it forces people into puerile self-interest, subjectivism and emotionalism; and it is wickedly presumptuous in its priestly bestowing of forgiveness and assurance.

It is certainly true that pastors and others will, at times, have to point out to believers the sin of an unforgiving spirit, and a host of similar problems arising from past 'hurts'. But the biblical method of pastoral care directs instruction, counsel and if necessary warning to the intelligent mind of sufferers, urging them to seek the help and forgiveness of God personally and directly.

What is wrong all of a sudden with direct prayer? Why can God no longer heal emotional wounds in answer to prayer? Why should *1 Peter 5.7* no longer be good enough — *Casting all your care upon him; for he careth for you*? Why should the fiction world of fantasising, role-play and pretence be elevated above believing prayer? And why should God have waited 2,000 years to reveal a 'better' method of healing to Seamands and company?

The answer to all these questions is that such ideas are just substitutes for real faith in the Lord and they are promoted by people who are capable of thinking that they know better than the Bible. Sometimes believers do suffer emotional afflictions which require very special help, but at no time should a pastoral counsellor play 'priest' or deep-analysis psychiatrist, claiming special inspiration from God, probing, play-acting, directing the 'patient' into a fantasy world, inventing words from Christ, and so on. This must be condemned as extra biblical and blasphemous, and all right-thinking believers must totally shun books which advocate such ideas.

Charismatic healers who encourage imagineering have no inhibitions about visualising the Lord Jesus in very great detail. The Rev Andy Arbuthnot, former head of a merchant bank, now an Anglican clergyman and resident healer at the London Healing Mission writes: 'I usually picture Jesus as a young man, and perhaps the first thing that strikes me is the peace which flows from Him . . . As we continue to look at Him, our eyes move upwards to His face. He has a dark skin . . . His hair is dark brown, almost black . . . '

To be fair to Mr Arbuthnot, he also attempts to include divine qualities such as holiness, love, power and compassion in his vision, but his overall aim is to try to capture the emotional sensation of having the Lord Jesus in the room with him, and this is what he wants his 'patients' to feel also. Instead of approaching the Lord *by faith* and *in trust*, the idea is to virtually reincarnate Him by the power of imagination, and to get as close as possible to feeling the impact of His physical presence.

Mr Arbuthnot's method is to meditate upon a Gospel narrative to achieve this almost total sense of the Lord's presence, but he is obliged to go way beyond the narrative. He proposes that one should read a passage several times, close the Bible and then proceed to imagine the event. He counsels us to — 'Go further, and fill in the details, the colour of the sky, the sandy track on which they were walking, the grey-green colour of the olive leaves . . . describe aloud . . . what Jesus is feeling throughout the episode, describe the expression on His face . . . the tone of His voice . . . so it will be possible to build up the image of Jesus in one's mind . . . one moves imperceptibly from the imagination into what is real.'

People who need their memories healed are encouraged to engage in the detailed visualisation of Jesus flogged and bleeding, 'with the blood clotted . . . and with black flies crawling all over the living flesh.' This will help them to accept the crucifixion as God's victory over all evil, darkness and suffering. Then sufferers must imagine Jesus coming down from the cross, resplendent in resurrection glory and power, and at this point Mr Arbuthnot will say to them, 'Put your right hand now into your heart; put it right into your heart and take out all the pain, all the hurt and all the sadness which is there. Take it out and see it, a nasty black mess in your right hand, and hand it over to Jesus.' It is claimed that sufferers say that as they do this in their imagination all the sorrow and sadness of wounded memories melt away until they fall like drops of pure water to the ground. People say, 'I actually felt the pain and the sadness leave me!'

If a person is assumed to be suffering from a child-hood hurt, then that person will re-live that childhood moment, and (in a shared flight of imagination) Mr Arbuthnot will lead them to the cross to gape upon it, and to experience Jesus coming down and healing them.

Mr Arbuthnot tells us how he often leads people into the wonderland of imagining spiritual events. He will speak to a patient in the following way: 'I see you as a little child of seven, getting up and walking round the table to Jesus. No, you're not walking, you're running. You're running to Jesus, and I can see you jumping, jumping on to His lap, and I can see you giggling with sheer joy as you snuggle in Jesus' arms. You look so gloriously happy there... you feel secure with His strong left arm around your shoulders, and as you lean back on His chest, you feel the warmth of His body, you can feel His heart beating, you look up into His smiling face... and you're just transported with utter joy.'

Imagineering of this sort has become a standard tech-nique with many charismatic workers, and we must, of necessity, ask the usual battery of questions. Where is it recorded that Paul or any other apostle worked in this way? How does all this match up to the second commandment?

Do such healing techniques honour the superscription which stands over all our relationships with the Lord — THE JUST SHALL LIVE BY FAITH? Is it *honest* to fantasise detailed fictional encounters with a physical Saviour, complete with dialogue and embraces? Is it not *blasphemous* to put words into the mouth of God, making Him say whatever we would like Him to say? Is it not grossly dangerous, sinful and fleshly to urge people (especially those who may be lonely and bereft of physical affection) to fantasise physical contact with the Lord of Glory, dwelling on attributes of manliness, protective strength, facial attractiveness, bodily warmth, and so forth?

Without doubt these techniques are unbiblical, but they are also blasphemous and carnal. They ruthlessly exploit the emotions of vulnerable people, cruelly adding to the religious delusions of those who suffer from neurotic afflictions, and further confusing their minds concerning the true and spiritual way of approaching Christ to obtain His blessing. The moment any professedly Christian worker spurns the Bible as the sole guide, authority and example for all pastoral methods, preferring instead these carnal imagineering techniques, such a person becomes a purveyor of fiction and fleshly delusion, and an enemy of Almighty God.

10
The Law of a Sound Mind
NT words insist on an alert, rational mind

IN THESE PAGES we have referred to a fundamental law of the Christian faith, that our rational minds must always be in control of our thoughts and actions, and that our minds must be wholly subservient to the Word of God as the exclusive source of authoritative teaching from God. The charismatic revolution has utterly flouted this law, which we call, *the law of a sound mind*, a term taken from Paul's words in *2 Timothy 1.7 — For God hath not given us the spirit of fear; but of power, and of love, and of a SOUND MIND.*

Charismatics claim that by maintaining rational control over our minds and actions we are opposing and quenching the work of the Holy Spirit. They say that believers *must* be prepared to surrender rational control in order that they may be open to direct divine activity in both worship and Christian service. John Wimber observes with concern that — 'Fear of losing control is threatening to most Western Christians.' He insists that we must overcome our fears, because rational control must be forfeited for tongues-speaking to occur; for soaring ecstatic sensations to be felt in worship; for messages from God to be received directly into the mind, and for miraculous events to happen, such as healings.

If divine healing is to take place, then gifted healers must launch away from sober, rational control so as to be open to 'words' from God, or 'TV' pictures in the mind, guiding them to diagnose disorders, and telling them what God intends to do for each sufferer. Increasing numbers of healers are practising the technique of putting sick people into trance states which knock out their power of rational control. The sufferer as well as the healer must surrender the rational faculty in order to obtain a blessing, supposedly from God.

Most charismatic healing meetings now begin with strenuous efforts to help people to surrender their rational control and behave in a completely uninhibited way. The goal is that worshippers should be 'open' to accept anything that happens, no matter how strange, inexplicable or bizarre it may be. Loud, rhythmic music forms the basis of worship, and all present are urged to join in with arm-waving, body-swaying, foot-tapping, and even dancing and leaping in the air. Rational control must at all costs be swept away because nothing which occurs must be impeded, tested or evaluated by the intelligent mind, versed in the Word of God.

By discarding the *law of a sound mind* (the protection provided by the reasoning faculty) charismatics have rendered themselves highly gullible in the face of false teaching, exaggeration and lies. They have become notably vulnerable to religious charlatans and rogues, as the 1987 crisis in American religious television (which is predominantly charismatic) has demonstrated. Emotionalism is rampant among them, and because all are free to do whatever seems right in their own eyes, serious spiritual lawlessness is widespread. These things are the inevitable result of laying aside the objective standard of God's Word, the faculty of judgement and the power of self-control, all of which are brought into play by the *safe mind*.

It is obvious that if traditional evangelical teaching is biblical in its insistence that the rational faculty must be kept switched on throughout our waking day then the entire charismatic scene is gravely out of order and opposed to the declared will of God. Can the traditional standard be proved from the Scripture? The incontrovertible fact is that the Bible teems with passages which state categorically that our duty is to maintain firm control of the mind in all our worship and other spiritual activities. So numerous and so emphatic are the commands to this effect that it is almost unbelievable that mature Christians still fall for the charismatic line that rational control is an impediment to the Spirit-filled life. We shall review a large number of 'unassailable' texts asserting the *law of a sound mind*, and then consider some of the reasons why the maintaining of a safe, rational mind is so strongly and constantly commanded in the Bible.

1. Safe-minded Words

The first group of texts to be considered contain the Greek word *sophron*, which in the *AV* is usually translated *sober*, sometimes *temperate*, and once *discreet*. The Greek word comes from *sozo* (to save) and *phron* (the mind) and literally means *safe in mind*. Therefore, to be *sober* (as used in the *AV*) generally means to be safe-minded, self-controlled, rational and sensible. It will be seen that Paul's use of this word condemns the main plank of charismatic thinking — that rational control must often be abandoned to get spiritual blessing.

In *1 Timothy 3.2* Paul states that elders must be men who at all times keep the rational faculty alert and in control. He says — A bishop then must be ... sober [SAFE IN MIND; SELF-CONTROLLED], of good behaviour [ORDERLY]. The safe-mindedness required of the elder is underlined by the Greek word for orderly, or well ordered. William Hendriksen shows that the impact of these words is that elders must always be 'moderate, well-balanced, calm, careful, steady and sane'. Does this leave scope for them to voluntarily renounce rational control? Of course not! The NIV translates the elder's required qualifications as temperate, self-controlled, respectable, and the NASB adds — prudent. The elder is to be a sagacious person, astute in mind, good at thinking, and endowed with discernment and mental penetration.

In Titus 1.8 Paul repeats the qualifications of elders, again using the Greek word safe-minded. (The AV translates it: sober, the NIV: self-controlled, the NASB: sensible.) In Titus 2.2 Paul extends this standard to all older men, commanding that they should be sober or safe-minded. Lest we should think that this safe-mindedness is only for office bearers and elderly men, Paul proceeds to command that the same applies to older women, and — that they may teach the young women to be sober (Titus 2.4). Young women also must be taught to be safe in mind (discreet in the AV), maintaining self-control both mentally and emotionally.

In Titus 2.6 Paul extends the standard still further, saying to Titus, Young men likewise exhort to be sober minded. Other translators say: self-controlled, sensible, prudent. (The precise Greek word here is sophroneo — to be in one's right mind; to be rational and safe in mind.) How can one possibly square this command with voluntary surrender of the control of speech, or the abandonment of oneself to trance states or self-induced 'trips' of emotional ecstasy?

Precisely the same word is used by Peter in his

command and instruction about true prayer: *Be ye therefore sober* [SAFE-MINDED; RATIONAL], *and watch unto prayer (1 Peter 4.7)*. The *NIV* translates it thus: *Therefore be clear minded and self-controlled so that you can pray*. Does this sound like a licence to pray in tongues, or to pray in response to wild visions and strange messages which are supposedly flashed into the mind? Prayer, according to Scripture, is an activity of a controlled, rational mind crying out to God in faith for blessing.

Another form of the *safe-minded* term appears in *Titus 2.12* — *Teaching us that, denying ungodliness and worldly lusts, we should live soberly, righteously, and godly, in this present world*. Here, *soberly* or safe-mindedly (Gk: *sophronos*) indicates self-restraint. The rational faculty is to maintain control over all our passions, thoughts and desires. God calls to worship Him a ransomed people who come into His presence with full control of their faculties and feelings. The Spirit will certainly lift us up to heights of spiritual love and worship, but we must never renounce our self-control. It is as image-bearers that we must worship God!

Other translations render *soberly* in this text by the following alternative terms: *sensibly; in a self-controlled way; with self-mastery*. The *sophron* family of words all contain the same elements — *safe* (or controlled, or restrained) *in mind*. Thus every one of the quoted verses testifies powerfully to the central place of the *over-conscious*, active, rational faculty in the life of the believer.

2. Self-control Words

Another highly important Greek word-group confirms the crucial importance of the believer maintaining conscious rational control of all his thoughts, words and deeds. This group consists of a verb, noun and adjective drawn from the word *kratos*, which means *strength, power* or *dominion*. All these words indicate *self-control*.

The verb *enkrateuo* is used by Paul in *1 Corinthians 9.25* when he speaks of the rigid self-control which is essential in the Christian life: *And every man that striveth for the mastery is temperate* [SELF-CONTROLLED] *in all things*. The *NASB* says — *exercises self-control in all things*. The athlete provides a perfect picture of the Christian. He never surrenders his rational self-control to impulses of diet or leisure, nor does he abandon his thought-out programme. The noun form of this word occurs in two key passages about sanctification. In *Galatians 5.23* this quality of rational strength or self-control is listed as part of the fruit of the Spirit — *temperance*. (Modern versions mostly say 'self-control'.)

In *2 Peter 1.5-6* self-control appears in the well-known chain for godly living. Peter says — *Giving all diligence, add to your faith virtue; and to virtue knowledge; and to knowledge temperance* [SELF-CONTROL]; *and to temperance patience; and to patience godliness*. Once again it is affirmed that believers must always be in control of their faculties. Firm rational control must never be switched off or bypassed for it is essential in the walk of holiness.

The self-control adjective occurs in *Titus 1.8-9*. We have already noted that the overseer must be *sober* or *safe-minded*, but Paul also says that he must be — *temperate* [SELF-CONTROLLED]; *holding fast the faithful word as he hath been taught, that he may be able by sound doctrine both to exhort and to convince the gainsayers*. He does not go into trances, nor does he expect direct communication from God by way of words of wisdom or knowledge. He keeps control of his reasoning, rational mind and he holds firmly to the Word of God which the apostolic generation has passed down to him.

He does not add to it; he simply teaches it. Thus by sound doctrine he exhorts those who contradict it. What an indictment these words are of those who have introduced extreme and wild doctrines which they claim have been given to them by visions, dreams and trances, while their rational functions were suspended.

The Greek verb *phroneo* (to *think*) is another word which indicates the controlling role of the mind in our affairs. It 'implies moral interest or reflection, not mere unreasoning opinion' (Vine). It speaks of the *directed* mind (and feelings), rather than the mind as a passive receptacle for information and impressions. The *phroneo* verb is used frequently by Paul as he commands us to apply our active, careful, controlling minds to spiritual objectives. Restricting ourselves to just one example, we choose *Colossians 3.2* — *Set your affection [phroneo* — MIND] *on things above, not on things on the earth.* The *NIV* and *NASB* both have *mind* (instead of *affection*), and the *MLB* captures the sense with — 'apply your minds' — *apply* being the operative word.*

The minds of believers must be ever active in evaluating and discerning the influences which constantly bombard them, and also in determining and directing all their words and actions. The rule of the New Testament is not a discarded or a dormant mind, but a sanctified, active, safe mind.

Set your affection is one word in Greek. Arndt & Gingrich translate it — 'set one's mind on; be intent on'. Godet notes that it is difficult to render the word *phroneo* (mind) into French or English 'because it includes at once *thinking* and *willing*'. Vincent comments: 'The verb primarily means *to have understanding*, then, to *feel* or *think* . . . to direct the mind to something.' [From Earle — *Word Meanings in the New Testament.*]

3. The Alert-minded Word

Another word which teaches the primacy of the rational mind is *nepho*, usually translated *sober* in the *AV*. It really means — free from the influence of alcohol — but in the New Testament it is plainly meant metaphorically, indicating that the mind must be clear and alert so that we can detect temptation or false teaching. Paul says in *1 Thessalonians 5.6* — *Therefore let us not sleep, as do others; but let us watch and be sober* [ALERT]. Everyone agrees that this is a metaphorical use of *sober*, and that Paul here exhorts us to be vigilant, and fully in control of our rational faculty.

In *1 Peter 1.13* the word is used in the same way, and also in *1 Peter 5.8-9* — *Be sober* [ALERT], *be vigilant; because your adversary the devil, as a roaring lion, walketh about, seeking whom he may devour: whom resist stedfast in the faith.* The frequently repeated standard of the Bible is — never switch off the rational, thinking, discerning faculty.

4. Thinking, Discerning, and Directing Words

Yet another Greek word for the mind or understanding is *dianoia*, which quite specifically refers to the exercised or thinking mind. The word strictly means — *a reflection* or *a thinking-through*. This term — *the thinking mind* — appears twice in Peter's epistles. In *1 Peter 1.13-14* we read: *Wherefore gird up the loins of your mind* [THINKING MIND] . . . *as obedient children.* In *2 Peter 3.1-2* we read: *This second epistle, beloved, I now write unto you; in both which I stir up your pure minds* [THINKING MINDS] *by way of remembrance: that ye may be mindful of the words which were spoken before by the holy prophets, and of the commandment of us the apostles of the Lord and Saviour.*

Peter does not tell us that we shall have visions or words of knowledge coming into our minds, but that our spiritual progress will depend on our thoughtful study of the inspired words of the prophets and apostles of the Lord. The principle is clear — God speaks as the Bible is channelled through our rational minds. The mind remains on duty in all our communion with the Lord also, for John declares — *And we know that the Son of God is come, and hath given us an understanding* [THINKING MIND], *that we may know him that is true (1 John 5.20).*

Luke records how the Lord instructed the disciples before He ascended into Heaven: *Then opened he their understanding* [nous — MIND], *that they might understand the scriptures (Luke 24.45).* This was to be the pattern for all communications of divine Truth once the New Testament was complete. This word for mind *(nous)* is described by Vine as denoting 'the seat of reflective consciousness, comprising the faculties of perception and understanding, and those of feeling, judging and determining.' Paul says — *I will pray with the spirit, and I will pray with the understanding* [NOUS] *also: I will sing with the spirit, and I will sing with the understanding also (1 Corinthians 14.15).*

We learn from this that the conscious, rational faculty is vital because the spirit (ie: the spiritual life) in a believer functions and expresses itself through this faculty. If the rational mind is switched off, it is not the spirit of a person which expresses itself, but merely the emotions.*

The Greek word *logizomai* means to *reckon*, to estimate, count up, or assess. In *1 Corinthians 13.11*

---

*Arndt & Gingrich say that *nous* 'denotes the faculty of physical and intellectual perception, then also the power to arrive at moral judgements'. It is such a faculty which co-operates with the spirit of a person in prayer and praise.

Paul says — *When I was a child, I spake as a child, I understood as a child, I thought* [RECKONED] *as a child: but when I became a man, I put away childish things*. To the adult Christian, the rational faculty assesses and evaluates all things all the time, in the light of the Bible alone. We are disobedient to the Lord if we allow ourselves to become mesmerised by the atmosphere worked up in charismatic meetings (usually by emotional and musical means), with the result that we cease to *reckon* or assess, and simply float along with the tide of unbiblical ideas and assertions.

The Greek word *suniemi* means *to bring together*. It is used metaphorically in the New Testament to describe the process of spiritual comprehension. If people grasp and perceive the meaning of a parable then this verb is used. For example, in *Matthew 13.51* Jesus asks the disciples, *Have ye understood* [*suniemi* — COMPREHENDED] *all these things?*

Paul reminds Timothy that it is by studying inspired words (like Paul's own) that he will get this quality of comprehension in all the things he needs to know. *2 Timothy 2.7* reads — *Consider what I say; and the Lord give thee understanding* [COMPREHENSION] *in all things.*** Timothy is not promised any way of getting divine knowledge other than by applying his mind to the inspired writings, which are good for *all things*. In *Colossians 2.2* Paul indicates that assurance flows out of deep comprehension of the Word. Charismatics seek assurance from signs and wonders, and from strange experiences, but Paul says — *That their hearts might be comforted . . . unto all riches of the full assurance of understanding* [COMPREHENSION]. In *Colossians 1.9-10* he prays that God's people — *might be filled with the*

**In this and the following text the noun *sunesis* (comprehension) is employed.

knowledge of his will in all wisdom and spiritual understanding [COMPREHENSION] ... *increasing in the knowledge of God.*

Always in Control

The New Testament is so full of exhortations to sound-mindedness, that it is simply impossible to do justice to them in a limited space. We may think of *Romans 12.2 — And be not conformed to this world: but be ye transformed by the renewing of your mind, that ye may prove what is that good, and acceptable, and perfect, will of God.* The intelligent, safe, sound mind both evaluates and appreciates all the spiritual things which God has for the believer.

In *Philippians 4.7-9* the believers' *minds* (as well as their hearts) are garrisoned by God so long as they keep them alert and ready to test all things. So Paul commands — *Finally, brethren, whatsoever things are true, whatsoever things are honest, whatsoever things are just, whatsoever things are pure, whatsoever things are lovely, whatsoever things are of good report; if there be any virtue, and if there be any praise, think on these things. Those things, which ye have both learned, and received, and heard, and seen in me, do: and the God of peace shall be with you.*

The role of the ever-awake rational faculty is yet again asserted by Paul in *2 Corinthians 10.5*, a verse which utterly condemns the uninhibited abandonment of the controlled mind which is so typical of charismatic experimentation: *Casting down imaginations, and every high thing that exalteth itself against the knowledge of God, and bringing into captivity every thought to the obedience of Christ.*

The standard has always been the same for true believers, as we see from David's words in *Psalm 32.9*

— *Be ye not as the horse, or as the mule, which have no understanding: whose mouth must be held in with bit and bridle, lest they come near unto thee.* Here the word *understanding* means — to distinguish or discern mentally; to think skilfully; to be prudent and wise.

Truly God has not given to us the spirit (ie: disposition or attitude) of timidity — *but of power, and of love, and of a sound mind (2 Timothy 1.7)*. In this text the Greek for *sound mind (sophronismos)* means a self-controlled or disciplined mind. All three dispositions are vital and precious to us as believers — the *power* to draw near to God and accomplish great things in His name; the capacity for *love*, and the *safe-mindedness* which controls and regulates all our thoughts and actions. The disposition and attitude which has produced today's charismatic healing methods is a disposition of spiritual abandon and adventure which is utterly contrary to the spirit of a sound mind commanded in the Bible. By abandoning the Scriptures, weighed and tested by the enlightened and rational mind, as their *sole* authority, charismatic healers have placed themselves at the mercy of a host of other influences, ranging from pure human imagination to demonic suggestion.

Made In the Image of God

The first biblical reason for insisting on the sanctity of rational control is that the reasoning mind is the faculty above all others which marks out human beings as those who are made in the image of God. Our status as image-bearers is revealed in *Genesis 1.26: Let us make man in our image, after our likeness: and let them have dominion over . . . all the earth.* The gift of reason is our highest and noblest faculty — the ability to think, discern and weigh things in a sensible, logical, organised and rational manner. Clearly, when man was first created he was a more glorious image-bearer than now. We have certainly lost the original innocence and unique spiritual compatibility with the Lord. In the garden of Eden our first parents could hear God's voice audibly, and talk with Him as we now speak to one another. But though the image has become gravely tarnished by the Fall, yet the human race continues to reflect the Creator in possessing moral awareness, an eternal soul, and a rational, reasoning faculty.

The chief end of man is to glorify God and to enjoy Him for ever, and we are to glorify Him as *image-bearers*, not as brute beasts. God does not summon the animal kingdom to call upon His name, to appreciate His attributes and to serve Him with all their hearts and minds. He calls only image-bearers to this privileged and glorious work. He calls those who possess a thinking, rational faculty, and who will use it to frame sincere expressions of gratitude, love and praise.

Men and women away from God have frequently sought to suppress this highest natural gift and to escape temporarily into a world of basic, animal emotions. Heavy drinking provides an opportunity to numb and dull the higher senses, so that the lower urges can prevail. Drunkenness is a short-term renouncing of reason; an abdication of the status of image-bearer; a desire to be rid — at least for a time — of the rational faculty. In the light of the phenomenon of drunkenness we must appeal to those who advocate charismatic ideas to consider what they are doing. The very aim and purpose of drunkenness is unwittingly shared by charismatics when they renounce their rational self-control and launch themselves like surfers on to waves of emotions, ecstasies, involuntary speech, random impressions, visions, hallucinations, messages in the head, fictional fantasising, and so on.

Genuine spiritual activity is the very opposite of drunkenness, as Paul indicates in the words of *Ephesians 5.18* — *Do not get drunk with wine, for that is dissipation, but be filled with the Spirit (NASB)*. The filling of the Spirit does not produce an alternative, alcohol-free form of emotional drunkenness! Not for a moment are the higher senses (the mind and reason) dulled or dimmed, so that the divine image in us is suppressed or bypassed. The very opposite is the case, because by the blessing of the Spirit our minds are given a far greater intelligence to grasp the breadth and length and depth and height, and to know the love of Christ which passes knowledge. Our praise is *all the more worthy* because it comes from people who are in full possession of their senses; who voluntarily and intelligently direct sincere and deeply felt sentiments of worship to their God and King.

Because the rational mind is the divine image upon us, it is intended to have an active and central role in all our affairs all the time. The Lord Jesus Christ declared: *Thou shalt love the Lord thy God with all thy heart, and with all thy soul, and with all thy mind (Matthew 22.37)*. We must no more switch off the thinking and controlling activity of our minds than the love of our hearts. To do so is an act of disobedience which renders us distasteful to the Lord. Therefore, because we are image-bearers, not animals, we must never lay aside the rational faculty, or allow ourselves to lose touch with reality. We must never do anything to impede the activity of this precious faculty. We must never render it insensible by drink, trance-like states, *voluntary* surrender to glossolalia, or by any other means.

We must never switch off the rational faculty in order to experience emotional trips (even when these are wrongly labelled as worship) or allow ourselves to be 'carried away' by Gospel rock music, or to swallow uncritically the tall stories of today's charismatic wonder-workers. In times gone by millions of people were persuaded to suspend their reasoning faculty and swallow the fables of medieval Rome, and this same kind of tendency has now re-appeared in the midst of charismatic evangelicalism.

The Mind is the Organ of Obedience

The vital importance of the rational mind is also obvious from the fact that it is the organ with which we hear, understand and obey God's will as revealed in the Bible. When the mind is renewed and illuminated by the Holy Spirit at conversion, we are enabled to receive by faith God's Word and to understand it. Then — says Berkhof — 'By the application of sanctified human reason to the study of God's Word man can, under the guidance of the Holy Spirit, gain an ever increasing knowledge of God.'

The Bible alone is God's Word; it is a completed revelation, and it is completely sufficient for all our spiritual needs. God gave all the Truth to the generation of the apostles (*John 14.26* and *16.13-15*). The completed Bible provides totally for the Lord's people, so that there is no doctrine or command which we need to receive which is not already in the Scriptures (*2 Timothy 3.16-17*).

This Bible must be diligently studied by our reasoning minds, because this is the *only* way that Christ will speak to us *authoritatively* until He shall come again. It is true that there are a number of incidental, subordinate ways by which God touches the hearts of His people, but *authoritative* guidance and teaching come only from His Word. As we have pointed out elsewhere, the Holy Spirit often prods our consciences and jogs our memories, moving us to acknowledge our sin, or to carry out a neglected duty. In His graciousness He will help us think clearly and biblically through difficult situations, but He will never give us revelations which bypass the process of studying His Word.

As we serve the Lord He may be the unseen Author of many ideas which we have for doing things more effectively. Therefore, if our minds become fertile and productive we shall certainly give Him all the glory. But because we cannot tell the difference between the Lord's prompting activity on our minds and our own imaginations, none of our ideas are *authoritative*, and we must never say, 'God told me, therefore I *will* do it.' All our thoughts must be brought humbly before the supreme principles of conduct given in the Bible, as God has commanded.

It is a grave violation of the *law of a sound mind* for people to allow their free-wheeling day-dreams to become the voice of God. How do they know that their 'messages' are not purely the product of their own imaginations? Some have detailed visions, but how do they know that they are not hallucinating? Almighty God has decreed that He will *never* put men and women in the position of not knowing whether their thoughts and dreams are messages from Heaven, or whether they are merely the fruit of their own random mental activity. He has categorically stated that He will speak doctrines and authoritative commands *only* by His Word, and He has commanded that we keep personal control over our minds as we study.

It is God Who has created the gift of reason, ennobled it, renewed it, anointed it, and He has commanded us to keep this faculty alert, in control, and subject *only* to the teaching of the Bible. Therefore, if a novel healing method is born in the mind of someone who says that God commanded it in a vision, or in a 'word of know-ledge', our suspicions *must* be aroused. Did God, after all, fail to finish the Bible? Is the proposed method in the Bible? The healer in question may seem to get impressive results, and susceptible fans may say that they feel the presence of the Spirit of God in his meetings, but the sole task of our reasoning mind is to ask — *What saith the scripture?* If it is not consistent with the clear teaching of the Bible, then it is not the will of God. At best it may be a grave mistake on the part of a well-meaning person who needs correcting; at worst, it may be the wilful invention of someone who is carnal, self-seeking and godless.

Because the mind is the essential organ of hearing and understanding God's will as revealed in the Bible, it must be at its most alert in times of worship and Christian service. To turn off rational control is to cut our lines of communication to God's will.

The Mind is the Palace of Faith

The mind or rational faculty is also of central importance to our Christian life because it is the residence or palace of *faith*. *Faith* is what we have when, by God's grace, the mind becomes fully convinced about God's words. We believe the teaching, the record of Christ's redemptive work, and the glorious promises of God. Because with our *minds* we have received the promises, we can rest our faith upon them. Our faith depends upon this reasoning faculty being enlightened by God and convinced of His Word. The New Testament word *faith* means — *persuaded*; *convinced*. Clearly we can only be *persuaded* or *convinced* if our minds are consciously functioning and open to God's Word. Therefore to switch off the mind is to undermine faith.

If we extinguish discernment and open our minds to unbiblical stories and dubious tales of daily miracles, what will be the furniture in the palace of faith? What will occupy the rooms of the mind? What will we be *persuaded* and *convinced* about? The mind must always guard its entrance doors and carefully label the stores which enter. Only God's Truth must be taken to the best room and *faith* will feed upon *these* stores. Other information may go into sundry side rooms and passages of the mind labelled as material to be inspected, evaluated and perhaps remembered, but never trusted or accepted as authoritative words sent from God.

In modern charismatic healing methods, the faith of those who seek healing is not placed in the Word of God, but in the claims and assertions of the healer. In the healing meeting, the celebrity healer says that you will be healed. He says he accomplishes this all the time. *He* (not the Bible) guarantees you a healing. Furthermore he claims to have received a word directly from God about you, saying what is wrong with you, and that it is about to be healed. He claims to have special power by way of a personal gift, so that people will fall backwards when he touches them. As the healing meeting proceeds, people all round the hall cry out and claim that they are being healed. Perhaps you have come to the meeting convinced that your reservations and misgivings must be laid aside as unworthy. You make yourself as open, susceptible and vulnerable to 'blessing' as possible by laying aside your rational faculty, the guard upon the door of your mind.

The result of all this is that your mind is filled with non-biblical information clamouring for your trust — information invented by the healer, *his* claims, *his* promises, *his* power, all reinforced by the plausible 'words of knowledge' which he speaks. What will your faith rest on now? As you seek a healing, your faith will be resting on a wild jumble of purely human assertions and claims; not on God's Word. Because the mind is the dwelling place of faith, we must never relax the duty of examining by the Word of God every teaching or idea which claims admission. The rational faculty must never go off duty, as the charismatics propose, because if it does, we shall be instantly vulnerable to human error and satanic subtleties.

Maturity Must Be Our Goal

The ultimate goal of our Christian life is conformity to Christ. In *Ephesians 4.13* Paul expresses this goal thus: *Till we all come in . . . the knowledge of the Son of God, unto a perfect man, unto the measure of the stature of the fulness of Christ.* We seek to deepen our character, grow in grace, increase in love and knowledge, and also in discernment and judgement. We are absolutely obligated to progress from spiritual childhood to spiritual maturity. Yet it must be said that the charismatic ideal is an abandonment of maturity and a reverting to childishness. The rhythmic pattern of music and dancing; the handclapping, the jolly informality, the uninhibited antics of some, together with the very low demands made on the *mind*, are all features of conduct which delight the very young and tend to embarrass the mature person.

Mature people are uncomfortable not because they are unwilling to let the Holy Spirit have sway in their lives (as the charismatics claim) but because they sense that this manner of proceeding is in the reverse direction from that of spiritual maturity.

As we seek to draw closer to Christ, and to be like Him, we must ask — was He abandoned in His behaviour? Did He encourage people to dance and jump and roll over on the ground (as some healers do today) before He healed them? Did He engage in uninhibited physical activities in His prayers to the Father? Did He put believers into trances or encourage them to shout

out suddenly, shriek, or cackle alarmingly? We are to imitate our Lord. We are on a journey to Christian maturity. We are commanded to exercise our adult minds and not to behave like children, who use their minds sometimes, and sometimes not. Our actions are always to be controlled, sincere, sensible and worthy of our Master.

Children love to pretend and play-act. They love stories and surprises. They are gullible, open, believing, and easily led astray. Our duty on the pathway of Christian maturity is clear from Paul's words — *When I was a child, I spake as a child, I understood as a child, I thought as a child: but when I became a man, I put away childish things (1 Corinthians 13.11).* How many believers allow themselves to be drawn into charismatic thinking through hearing stories of how people have supposedly been restored by a 'gifted' healer, but they do not ask — *What saith the scripture?* Sadly, this reflects the difference between a child and an adult. The little child is amazed at what the conjurer can do, whereas the adult perceives that things are not always what they seem, and applies certain laws to the situation.

We hear even of ministers who have been drawn into charismatic pastors' fraternals and conferences where they have thrown off the mantle of maturity to experiment with the claim that uninhibited behaviour releases the blessing of the Spirit. It is the ultimate tragedy when worked-up emotional sensations have to take the place of genuine power and blessing from God. The road to Heaven has always led upwards, not downwards, and this goes for maturity of behaviour, rational control and discernment as well as for all the other objectives of the Christian life. Paul underlines the issue with the words — *Brethren, be not children in understanding . . . but in understanding be men (1 Corinthians 14.20).*

By abandoning the duty of spiritual maturity and the law of a sound mind charismatic teachers have plunged thousands of believers into the very quagmire of childish, superstitious religion which true Christianity lifts us above. With supposed healings as its principal 'selling point' charismania reverts the process of maturity, turning people into mere children — *tossed to and fro, and carried about with every wind of doctrine, by the sleight of men, and cunning craftiness, whereby they lie in wait to deceive (Ephesians 4.14).*

11
A Medical View of Miraculous Healing
by Professor Verna Wright MD FRCP

AS A PHYSICIAN, my primary interest is in rheumatology, which concerns a chronic disease in many sufferers, and I have numerous patients whom I have followed over the years. I am also a Christian who believes the Bible in its totality, and who believes in the person and the work of the Holy Spirit. My work takes me to many parts of the world, and I have endeavoured to examine the subject of divine healing wherever I have gone. When we speak about divine healing in the present context we are speaking of what is commonly termed the *miraculous*. The *Shorter Oxford English Dictionary* says that a miracle is a marvellous event exceeding the known powers of nature, and therefore supposed to be due to the special intervention of the Deity or of some supernatural agency. In the case of healing, a miracle is defined as an event which exhibits control over the laws of nature and which serves as evidence that the agent is either divine or specially favoured by God.

There is no question of course that God *can* heal in a miraculous way, and there is no question that God *did* heal in a miraculous way in Bible times. I have no doubt at all that the man with the withered arm had his arm perfectly restored at the command of the Lord Jesus. What we are asking ourselves is, does God heal according to this miraculous fashion today, as a general procedure? The cry today is, 'Of course! Jesus is the same yesterday, today and forever.' I believe this scripture; but I must take seriously the *sense* in which Christ is always the same. He is the same *in person* but not necessarily *in purpose*. There is a time, there is a place, there is a purpose.

If I were to collect Moses' rod (and I suppose if I went to enough Catholic churches I might gather sufficient relics to do so) and if I were to extend this rod over the Red Sea and then walk, that would be a recipe for a watery grave. There was a *time*, there was a *place*, there was a *purpose*. The children of Israel walked forty years through the wilderness, yet their clothes never wore out, they did not need new shoes, their food was provided miraculously every morning, and as they walked in obedience to God no diseases came upon them. However, I do not think that if I went for a forty year walk in the Sinai desert today I would have no need to replenish my clothes, visit the cobbler or provide my daily bread, nor do I think that I would be untouched by surrounding diseases. There is a *time*, there is a *place*, there is a *purpose*.

There is one sense in which all healing is divine. How would an incision that a surgeon has made heal up but for the fact that there is an overruling God Who orders things in such a way? I recognise that in one sense all healing comes from God, but we are considering whether *evidently miraculous* healing is God's normal manner of healing Christians today. I take grave issue with the suggestion that all may be miraculously healed provided they have sufficient faith. I wish to submit to you that it is not true to Scripture, it is not true to experience and it is damaging in the extreme.

Some Medical Considerations

Permit me to comment on a number of medical aspects which it is important to appreciate if we are to evaluate the claims for healing that abound on every hand. The first factor is the *language of doctors*. One night after I had preached in an evangelical church in Leeds, a lady came up to me, warmly shook my hand and said, 'Professor, I came to hear you tonight because I am a patient of yours and the arthritis in my hand is completely gone. It was a miracle.' So it was, in the sense that God had performed a healing process in her life, but I am not able to say that it was a miracle in the sense that we have laid down — *a marvellous event exceeding the known powers of nature*, etc. There are many patients who come into my consulting room who have improved far more quickly than I might have anticipated from the treatment given. In these circumstances a doctor might loosely say to the patient, 'My dear, it is a miracle,' but he does not mean a miracle in the sense just defined, but rather in the sense that the condition has responded to treatment or has gone into spontaneous remission more quickly than he would have anticipated. The patient may well go away and say absolutely accurately, 'The doctor said it was a miracle.' However, if the patient thinks it is a miracle in the sense that we are speaking about then the patient does not appreciate the language of doctors.

The second factor we must take account of in evaluating miraculous healing is *how patients perceive their illness*. I teach my medical students that there are three things patients tell you that you can never believe. First, how much alcohol they drink. Secondly, whether they have had venereal disease, and thirdly, what the 'other' doctor said. You would be amazed what people believe the doctor has said. An interesting study of this was made at the London Hospital Rheumatology Clinic where interviews with patients were tape-recorded (with their permission). Immediately afterwards patients were questioned about the content of those interviews. There was one patient, a relatively young person, who was reassured by the doctor that the symptoms of which she complained were not serious arthritis and so the outlook was very good. She went out of the consulting room and within two minutes was interviewed, one of the questions being, 'What did the doctor say was the outlook?' 'Oh,' she replied, 'he said I would be crippled by the time I was forty.' This lady had gone into the consulting room with an idea in her mind and nothing was going to shift it. She was absolutely sincere in what she reported, but there was objective evidence that she was utterly wrong.

Patients often fail to understand the nature or the degree of seriousness of their condition. Let me give you an example from an Anglican church which placed a good deal of emphasis upon the healing ministry. A lady from this church who suffered from abdominal pain told the church prayer group that she was going into hospital the following week for extensive surgery. Naturally they prayed for her. She came out of hospital some fourteen days later and reported to the group that the operation had revealed that the disease had entirely disappeared, and they praised the Lord for this great deliverance.

It so happened that there was a surgeon in the congregation, a man clearly sympathetic to the healing movement, or he would not have been there. With the patient's permission he obtained sight of the medical notes and discussed them with the surgeon who performed the operation. He found that the surgeon had been extremely reluctant to operate and had only been persuaded to do so because of great pressure from the patient and her general practitioner. He opened the abdomen and rather as he anticipated he found nothing but a rather mobile colon. He therefore sewed the lady up again and her abdominal pain disappeared, but she soon began to suffer from migraine with increasing severity. Note the difference of perspective: to the healing group this was a miracle. Did they not have the testimony of the patient? She suffered from abdominal pain and extensive surgery was going to be necessary to rectify it; they prayed for her, the surgeon operated, and nothing could be found. But from the surgeon's perspective a very different story emerged, and we may feel that it was significant that this lady's symptoms soon changed from abdominal pain to migraine.

The third factor we must consider is the *difficulty of measuring responses in healing*. I head a clinical research team at the University of Leeds, where the measurement of response is an area of particular interest. How do you measure the response of people? Obviously there are subjective symptoms, but these are naturally difficult to measure because they depend entirely on what the patient says, and we have to devise visual analogue scales in order to evaluate what is said. A prime example of this is pain, which is a subjective symptom, as reflected in the lines —

> *There was a faith-healer of Deal,*
> *Who said, 'Although pain isn't real,*
> *When I sit on a pin*
> *And it punctures my skin,*
> *I dislike what I fancy I feel.'*

Then there are what we may call semi-subjective symptoms, that is, symptoms which have an objective element but are influenced by subjective factors. I am particularly interested in strength of grip and have carried out work to show that the strength of grip of rheumatoid patients is very weak first thing in the morning and that it increases as the day goes on. It is interesting to observe the subjective factors that come into strength of grip, because one might easily suppose that this is an objective measurement. The patient, after all, just squeezes the pneumatic dynamometer, you watch the column of mercury and take your reading. But the measurement of grip is not wholly objective; it is semi-subjective. To give an example, when Arab weight-lifters lift their weights, at a certain point they shout, 'Allah!' and up goes the weight. This is not merely a pious exclamation but it actually helps them to perform better. An experiment has been carried out in which someone was squeezing a dynamometer when a revolver was let off behind them, and it was amazing how much higher the grip reading went!

There are also entirely objective ways of measuring medical factors, but I wish to emphasise some of the difficulties of objective measurement. We are frequently quoted instances of leg-lengthening by miraculous means. This is an area in which I am interested because there is a type of arthritis that you can have if you have a disparity in the length of leg; we call it long-leg arthropathy. I know a church where a person came out thrilled because a leg had been seen to grow half an inch. However, it is impossible to measure accurately a difference of half an inch in the leg. I have tried for years to do it, and you cannot do it, not even with X-rays. So if anyone says, 'I saw a leg grow half an inch,' whatever you may say to them, you may dismiss that from your mind. It cannot be done scientifically.

As far as leg length disparity is concerned there are a number of factors that cause this. There is *true*

shortening of the leg, and there is *apparent* shortening.
A person may suffer an apparent shortening of the leg
by a tilt of the pelvis, and so we have to recognise that
what may appear to be a lengthening of the leg in these
circumstances, would really be a matter of the pelvis
getting on to an even keel.

In a Baptist church attended by a member of my
family there was a lady with backache. She went to a
John Wimber healing meeting and returned thrilled
because her backache had been cured. My relative
enquired about the means and was told, 'Well, someone
laid hands on me and told me that my backache was due
to a difference in my length of leg, and that if I went
home and measured my legs I would find that they were
of equal length and my backache would go.' The lady
went home and, surprise, surprise, when she measured
her legs they were of equal length. That is not a bad
way, I may say, of achieving results. The patient was, of
course, unaware of any supposed difference before. I
regret to say that follow-up of the patient revealed that
in three months her pain had returned. The difficulties
which we have in the measurement of response must be
well understood for they are relevant to any medical
consideration of healing claims, the majority of which I
believe to be spurious.

The fourth factor which we must consider is *mistakes
in diagnosis* of illnesses. You may have read of a lady
who in 1986 was awarded £94,000 damages in the High
Court because a bilateral mastectomy operation had
been performed on her, that is, both her breasts had
been removed. The reason was she had a lump which
was thought to be cancer and therefore the operation
was performed. The diagnosis was not just based on
clinical examination. A frozen section of tissue had been
prepared and examined under the microscope, but
despite this a mistaken diagnosis was made and the lady

was ultimately £94,000 the richer.

Such mistakes can be to a doctor's extreme embarrassment as well as to the patient's discomfort. Two years ago I had come to see me a man in his late sixties who had developed jaundice, was itching all over and had lost three stone in weight. I was very concerned and brought him into hospital immediately. Amongst our investigations was an ultrasound of his abdomen and the result showed that he had cancer of the liver with secondary deposits. I went to see the department concerned to check up on this result because it was obviously so sinister and important. However, I was assured that with modern technology the result was beyond any shadow of doubt. Imagine my mixture of delight and embarrassment when a year later the patient came to my clinic, all his symptoms having disappeared. The mistake was in the diagnosis. We must not think that doctors are infallible.

Alexis Carrel in his book *Voyage to Lourdes* tells how he saw at Lourdes an abdominal tumour disappear. He tells us that it would have impressed him greatly but for the fact that he had trained at Charing Cross Hospital where Mr Norman Lake the surgeon used to tell the story of a patient who had an 'elusive' and painful abdominal tumour. Four times they had taken the patient to theatre, and each time as soon as they put the patient under the anaesthetic the tumour disappeared. On the fourth occasion they decided to go ahead with the operation, and when they opened the abdomen the surgeon was just in time to see a volvulus of the large intestine unwinding. A volvulus is when an organ of the body twists on itself. This man obviously had a mobile large bowel which had twisted on itself, giving abdominal pain and creating a swelling or tumour. The surgeon saw what had obviously happened on previous occasions — with the relaxation brought about by the anaesthetic this volvulus had unwound.

A fifth factor to bear in mind is *the variability of disease*. There are striking spontaneous remissions even amongst cancer sufferers on rare but well-documented occasions. I am at the moment writing a book with another doctor on rheumatic diseases. I was very distressed some while ago to learn that my colleague was unable to write at that moment because of an attack of multiple sclerosis. There were speech difficulties, difficulty in writing and general illness. In fact, some years before in South Africa, there had been an initial episode which had cleared up completely, but this time it was of considerable severity. I was absolutely delighted a few months later to learn that all these symptoms had once again cleared completely and my colleague was able to deliver the expected part of the book only a little behind schedule. We must appreciate that there is a natural variability in disease.

A sixth, very significant factor is *the power of the psyche*. So often patients say to me, 'Is it my nerves, doctor?' I am careful how I answer that question because if I simply replied, 'Yes,' they might think that I was telling them that they were imagining it. I do not believe that pain is imaginary. If patients have pain, they have pain. I teach my medical students that everyone who crosses the threshold of the surgery has something wrong with them even if there appears to be nothing wrong with them. I do not believe that pain is imaginary. However, there is no question that if one is 'strung up' or tense, then this tension may manifest itself in physical symptoms. I know that when I am under a lot of pressure I get an aching around the neck. Psychological factors can manifest themselves as physical disease, and indeed in most physical diseases there is a psychological *component*.

Again, let us take rheumatoid arthritis; there is no

question, that this is a real, physical, inflammatory, sometimes destructive, joint disease. And yet if there is a bereavement in the family or if there is some tension or upset such as the husband leaving home, the patient will often suffer a flare up of symptoms; an exacerbation.

Or take the question of asthma. We recognise that in this disease there is often a *predisposing cause*, it may be of an hereditary nature, but there are three major components: infection, allergy and the psychological. So if a patient gets a cold, he may develop an asthmatic attack. In certain seasons of the year, because he is allergic to certain pollens, he may get an asthmatic attack. But there is a psychological component as well. This is well illustrated by an incident that happened at Liverpool, where I trained. There was an asthmatic sufferer who was allergic to roses and always went into an asthmatic attack if she visited a rose garden. She came into the consulting room of my chief, who happened to have a rose on his desk, and she promptly had an asthmatic attack. It was in fact a plastic rose. It is clear that the psychological aspect of disease should not be underestimated.

The psychological aspect is of tremendous importance when we come to analyse what is happening in certain healing meetings. When the John Wimber team conducted a healing meeting in Leeds, five of my colleagues (Christian doctors) were present. They were so incensed by what they saw that they afterwards wrote an account of their reactions. I will quote to you what they said.

There was an hour's repetitious chorus singing which began the proceedings. A fair amount of reeling and writhing commenced at the start of the singing. No space was found for a Scripture reading as such. The congregation was at no time called to prayers of confession of sin and repentance. 'Hold out your hands. Feel heat coming through you. Your eyelids may feel heavy. You may feel like falling; some persons may scream. It is all right. You can see the Holy Spirit resting on people, the power of God resting on many.'

Subjects for the team's healing ministry were gathered from the audience by a team member who took the microphone to broadcast his word of knowledge. There were descriptions of symptoms or illnesses that were being suffered by persons present. Those so described were asked to step forward. The list of conditions was general enough for the description to fit several in any group of five hundred or more.

The volunteers were then put into trance while hands were laid on them. They were not unconscious and would, we were assured, hear what was said to them. They remained thus for many minutes with assorted shakings, tremblings, smilings, fallings, swayings and utterings. Their various features were then exhibited to the congregation. We were assured that the smile here and the posture there were clearly visible evidence that the Holy Spirit had descended.

Throughout the building other individuals proceeded to fall into trance. The audience was told that the Holy Spirit might lead some persons to scream or to breathe very deeply. As one expected from hypnotic states these things happened more or less at once. Uncontrollable laughter, crying, groaning, shrieking and sobbing, together with the murmurings of many who wished to minister some spiritual comfort to the affected brethren made it more difficult to follow any more the official progress of events.

Amplified voices of team members came through,

'It is increasing everywhere. Give us more, Lord. Break that bondage. Release their hearts. Set them free. Relax.'

All five of the doctors, one of whom is one of this country's leading psychiatrists, described this as hypnosis. Indeed the psychiatrist said it was 'a very expert performance containing all the textbook characteristics of the induction of hypnosis.' The conclusion of my colleagues was this:

Hypnotic trance with suggestion is a powerful psychological tool. It has many uses. Psychosomatic disorders and physical symptoms related to neurosis are very likely in the short term to respond to this treatment. Relief of pain as in dental extraction or childbirth is relatively commonplace with hypnosis. In the Wimber team's meeting we saw no change that suggested any healing of organic, physical disease. Given the concern of many attenders to be of use to their neighbours some very helpful suggestions were undoubtedly made during the numerous trance states.

The hypnotic state, though conscious, is not what Scripture means by self-control, the mind of Christ in us or mind renewal. To describe these trances, their visible or audible features, or any healings experienced as the perfectly legitimate result of hypnosis — to describe this as the plain work of the Holy Spirit is a deception. To encourage techniques which produce hypnosis and hysteria and to teach that one is learning how to exercise kingdom rule over demons, disease and nature is false; it is misrepresentation.

I cannot emphasise my agreement with this conclusion too strongly.

Medical Surveys of Faith Healing

All the detailed analyses which have been made of healing claims over the years have failed to produce evidence of cures being achieved except for the kind of disorders which in medicine we call *functional* states. Much of this is discussed in an excellent book published by the Christian Medical Fellowship entitled *Some Thoughts on Faith Healing*, edited by Edmunds and Scorer.

Perhaps one of the earliest investigations of miraculous healing undertaken in this century was an Anglican commission headed by nine eminent Anglican clerics assisted by eleven doctors. Their conclusion was this. They acknowledged that no sharply defined fundamental distinction could be drawn between organic illness (in which there are structural changes in organs) and functional ailments (in which there is no change in structure, but the illness has a psychological cause). However, they were forced to the conclusion that faith and spiritual healings, like all treatment by suggestion, could be permanently effective only in cases of what are generally called *functional* disorders and that the alleged exceptions are so disputable that they cannot be taken into account.

In 1920 Canon Grinstead of Oxford looked into the results of two healing missions conducted by Anglican clergymen, and reported that letters sent to every doctor and clergyman in the district concerned failed to produce any information of definitely organic cases being healed, though there was plenty of evidence for the cure of *functional* disorders.

Again, the British Medical Association conducted a survey much more recently. They employed a well-advertised questionnaire which was sent to a large number of doctors and organisations devoted to the task of faith or spiritual healing, and they set up an interviewing committee chaired by a much-respected and very fair-minded consultant. They sifted all the evidence and this is what their report concluded:

> We find that whilst patients suffering from psychogenic disorders may be cured by various methods of spiritual healing, just as they are by methods of suggestion and other forms of psychological treatment employed by doctors, we can find no evidence that organic diseases are cured solely by such means.
>
> The evidence suggests that any such cases claimed to be cured are likely to be either instances of wrong diagnosis, wrong prognosis, remission, or possibly of spontaneous cure. On the other hand, as there are multiple factors, whether of body or mind, which may contribute to the precipitation of an illness, so there are multiple factors which are conducive to the restoration of health. Religious ministration on whatever basis it rests may have an important bearing upon the emotional and spiritual life of the patient and so contribute to recovery.

We could quote survey after survey in the same vein. Dr Louis Rose, a consultant psychiatrist at St Bartholomew's Hospital, looked at this issue over a period of twenty years. Professor John Dundee, the Professor of Anaesthetics at Queen's University, Belfast, recently looked at cases claimed to have received healing through the Centre for Christian Renewal. He looked at thirty-two cases in all and he came to the following conclusions:—

> As a result of this survey I would commend rather than criticise the role of the Church in healing the whole person. I failed to find undisputed evidence of miraculous healing, but I did meet patients who were

improved in mind and spirit. The doctor in the providence of God can help the body, the psychiatrist can help the mind, and I believe in the concept that the mind can affect the actions of the body in this life and the fate of the soul eternally.

Professor Dundee sees the role of the Church in that context, and so do the other surveys which we have referred to. More recently my friend Duncan Leighton, an evangelist, obtained a Kodak travelling scholarship to go to Africa and America. He wrote an article entitled, *Signs? One Wonders*, in which he tells of his own investigations of miraculous healings:

> In Africa in 1984, I followed the Derek Prince team through Zambia where they claimed thousands of miracle healings. We found none. Dr Eric Rea examined one miracle leg-lengthening and pronounced it a hoax. My letter asking Mr Prince for detailed information was passed down the line until it reached Brian Bentley who knew someone whose sinus was cured.

Duncan Leighton then went to California where he looked at some of the healing groups there. Roger Ziegler, a Californian chiropractor who is a Christian man, said after one healing meeting, 'Almost half the bad backs I deal with have already been healed in this place.'

This is the kind of testimony we receive from those who have looked objectively and sympathetically at healing claims over a long period of time. We must therefore, by way of medical considerations, appreciate the meaning of doctors when they loosely describe remission as 'a miracle'. We must also appreciate the possibility that patients may have misunderstood what has actually been said about their condition. We need to appreciate the difficulty of the measurement of response. We must understand the mistakes made by doctors in diagnosis. We have to understand something of the variability of diseases, even those which seem the most sinister, and we must never underestimate the power of the psyche.

Jesus Christ is the same yesterday, today and forever *in person* but not always *in purpose*, and the evidence which I have personally amassed certainly suggests that His purpose in these days is very different from His purpose in Bible times. There were good reasons of course why in the days of His flesh we needed the authentication of Who He was, and likewise we needed authentication of apostles as the heralds of the Gospel.

'Healings' Which Discredit Christ

I am certain that the person who claims to have a gift of healing discredits the person of Christ, because if (and it is a big 'if') there were ninety-nine successes and only one failure, even that would discredit Christ, because He *never* fails. If we say to a man, 'In the name of Jesus rise up and walk,' and he continues to lie at the Beautiful Gate of the Temple, that is a failure which reflects upon the person and the power of Christ, and this is happening all the time.

At a college near to my home there is a Christian Union in which the charismatic view has gained increasing sway. A girl who was a member of this Christian Union fractured her ankle and was also smitten with chickenpox. She was taken into the sick bay where some members of the committee went to visit her, prayed over her, assured her she was healed, and smuggled her out of the window of the sick bay. But by the time she had crossed the field to her living quarters she was so ill that they had to take her back again to the sick bay. What does this kind of activity do to the cause of Christ?

In my department, because my colleagues know that I am a Christian, when patients come to the clinic who claim to have experienced miraculous healing, they usually refer them to me saying, 'We thought you would like to see this case, Prof.' One of the last patients to be referred to me in this way was a lady with rheumatoid arthritis, who told my Senior Registrar that she had been healed at the Dales Bible Week. I said to her, 'Well, that is very interesting.' Obviously it is not my place as a doctor to pour doubt and scorn on these things. I then said, 'May I just look at your hands?'

Rather shamefacedly the lady stretched out her hands, but they were so gnarled and deformed that it was incredible. Some of the activity of the rheumatoid disease had abated, there was no question about that, but the deformity and destruction was evident for all to see — remarkably different I may say from the healings of the Lord Jesus. This sad situation rather reminded me of the cowman in the milking shed whom the farmer, to his surprise, saw pouring the milk back into the feed trough. He asked the cowman what he was doing, and the cowman said, 'Well, it looked rather weak so I thought I would put it through again.' I felt rather like that with this poor lady, thinking that she could do with being put through again.

When John Wimber's team visited Leeds a girl with deep psychiatric problems fell down screaming and she was declared to be healed, but three months later she was in a psychiatric hospital. So many of the success stories which we hear amount to reporting from a distance, but the physicians on the spot see a different picture. Those who have read Canon Michael Green's book *I Believe in the Holy Spirit* will know that he quotes instances of healing in Africa, in places where there had been great healing meetings. You may be interested to know the views of a missionary doctor who had been working in that area for many years. He wrote:

During my career in this country from 1944, there have been many reported healings, particularly in the area on both sides of Lake Nyasa, now called Lake Malawi. The 1973 outbreak in the Dar es Salaam area was the only one which I have heard of outside the Lake Nyasa area. All the outbreaks I have come across have followed the same pattern, that is, tremendous popularity initially with thousands of people being attracted to the meetings, followed by gradual thinning out of the attendances. When the popularity has waned the outbreak ends and the organisers move to another area. My own impression is that there is nothing to these healings, and that the initial popularity of the meetings decreases as the actual results become known. I have not come across a single case of undoubted cure proved by medical examination of the clinical condition before and after the alleged healing.

That was the impression of someone who was on the spot, and therefore I wish to emphasise that spurious claims discredit the person of Christ. Not only that, but they undermine the authority of God's Word. How many of us were saddened that David Watson's testimony was so marred by the fact that on radio broadcasts he said not once but two or three times, 'The one thing that encourages me is that all around the world the prophets have said this sickness is not unto death.'

So often, in my experience, the 'healings' of the charismatic movement are bound up with such words of prophecy and words of knowledge. I quote from the John Wimber meeting in Leeds: 'You receive a word of knowledge; God wants you to speak it out loud. You make some mistakes, never mind, go for the next one!' How unscriptural and extraordinary that is, but those very words were said. This is not being said behind the back of the John Wimber team because the day following the meeting in question there was a gathering for Christian leaders and ministers and some of my medical colleagues went along to express their strong reservations about what was happening. When they did so they were told that it was wrong to use the mind to assess these matters. What Christians needed, it was said, was to feel the touch of God. However, we must assert that to bypass the mind in such a way is to discredit the Word of God and to undermine its authority.

Listen to some words of Jonathan Edwards about people who rejected the spirit of discernment:

They looked upon critical enquiries into the difference between true grace and its counterfeits, or at least being very busy in such enquiries and spending time in them, to be impertinent and unseasonable; tending rather to damp the work of the Spirit of God than promote it; diverting their own minds and the minds of others, as they supposed, from that to which God at such an extraordinary time did loudly call them more especially to attend. The cry was, 'Oh, there is no danger, if we are but lively in religion and full of God's Spirit and live by faith, of being misled! If we do but follow God there is no danger of being led wrong! Let us press forward and not stay and hinder the good work by standing and spending time in these criticisms and carnal reasonings!' This was the language of many, until they ran on deep into the wilderness, and were caught by the briars and thorns of the wilderness.

I could not endorse that too strongly. When unwarranted claims of miracles are not properly assessed, the person of Christ is discredited, the Word of God is undermined, Christians are deceived, and a race of gullible believers is bred. I cannot for the life of me understand how there can be a platform exercising a healing ministry when many of those who occupy it wear glasses. Smith Wigglesworth, the great healer of a bygone day, called them eye-crutches, and so they are.

Again, just to emphasise the gullibility connected with charismatic healing, I turn to another incident which occurred at a college Christian Union. The president, who was much inclined to these views, arrived at the weekly Bible study having had 'flu very badly, and was now streaming with cold. The young man was clearly very sick, but he assured everyone about his condition with these words: 'I want to tell you that God has healed me, but the devil is keeping the symptoms there.' This is the terrible gullibility that we are encouraging, especially among young Christians.

I would like to say to these miracle healers, 'Pray tell me, why are you not found in the hospices?' Similarly, I would like to say to the prosperity prophets, 'Pray tell me, why are you not found in Ethiopia, in the Sudan or in India where I have met many who are impoverished in this world's goods but have a spiritual richness that makes me feel like a pauper?'

The Cruelty of Miracle Healing

Apart from the damage which the miraculous healing movement is doing to the faith, it is a *cruel teaching* because by claiming that all may be healed if they have sufficient faith, it increases the agony of many who are sick. At Horsforth, on the edge of Leeds, Don Double conducted a healing crusade. Mr Double heals different ailments on different nights and it so happened one night he was healing the deaf, and a friend of mine who is deaf in one ear thought he would have a go at being healed. Hands were laid upon him and he was told that he was healed, but he said, 'I am not.' The healer said, 'Yes you are.' My friend insisted, 'No, I am not,' only to be told, 'Well it must be that you have not got sufficient faith.' After a brief altercation the healer went on down the line of deaf people. When the healing activities had finished my friend turned to the lady next to him and said, 'What did it do for you, love?' and she replied with her hand cupped to her ear, 'What did you say?'

We may be amused by such stories, but there are times when it can be very distressing. Once I was leading an evangelistic team on the Isle of Man and we had with us a young fellow from a Bible College who suffered from epilepsy. He had fallen in with this miraculous healing teaching and as a result had abandoned his medication. During the night, sleeping like the rest of us on a camp bed, he had a major epileptic fit in the course of which he urinated over his bed. Of course there is no shame in that, but how terribly embarrassing for the poor chap. It was not his fault at all; it was the folly of those who had told him he had been healed.

But the consequences of such assurances can be even more distressing, and very damaging also. I have other friends whose eleven-year-old son died of leukaemia, but this couple had been promised and assured of healing for their child and they had both believed that promise deeply. Their distress was almost intolerable.

I think of a church where a couple had a child who was severely afflicted and disabled with cystic fibrosis. Cystic fibrosis is caused by a recessive gene, which means that it must be carried by two partners. If two such people marry there is a strong chance of the offspring having cystic fibrosis. The couple went to the doctor to ask about a future family and the doctor advised against it, explaining that there was a one in four chance that other children would be affected. They reconciled themselves to the situation. One day in their church someone stood up with a word of knowledge and said, 'You will have a normal child.' So they had a child, but it was more severely affected than the first, and they have since been looking after a most disabled child.

I think of a church in which a childless couple had come to terms with their situation, having been investigated fully and informed that they could not have children. Naturally they were very desirous of having children. One day somebody stood up in the fellowship and claimed to have a word of knowledge: 'Within twelve months you will have a child.' Eighteen months elapsed; the couple were still childless and the pastor of the church had to devote hours of pastoral time in counselling two believers whose Christian faith had been shattered by this so-called word of knowledge.

William Nolan was a distinguished surgeon in the USA, a very caring man who signed on as a helper for the famous healing meetings of the late Kathryn Kuhlman. He went with an open mind, his desire being to help. Ultimately he was to leave the organisation and to write a book entitled, *Healing: A Doctor in Search of a Miracle*. This is what he wrote.

I had mixed emotions about the follow-up study. On the one hand I felt that Kathryn Kuhlman was a sincere, devout, dedicated woman who believed fervently that she was doing the Lord's will; I did not want to hurt her. On the other hand I was not sure that whatever good Miss Kuhlman was doing was not far outweighed by the pain she was causing. I could not get those crippled and idiot children and their weeping, broken-hearted parents out of my mind, and all the others cruelly disappointed.

Such conclusions could be justifiably repeated again and again. But it is necessary to say that this miraculous healing teaching is not only damaging, it is often *disastrous*. I think of a general practitioner who was a great friend of mine, a fine Christian lady who had led many people to Christ, but she suffered from severe depression. Fortunately her depression was controlled by medication. Her counselling ministry was one that I valued so much that I would often send my depressed patients to her for help. Unfortunately she fell in with a group who majored on this miraculous healing teaching, and she was informed that she had been healed. She therefore abandoned her medication, but three weeks later she hanged herself.

I think of another person, a girl from Leeds, who had severe epilepsy, but fortunately she was controlled on medication. She too fell in with a similar charismatic group, and likewise she abandoned her medication. One day she travelled over to Harrogate, stepped off a bus, had a major epileptic fit and fell under the wheels of an oncoming car to be killed outright. I put the deaths of those two useful Christians firmly and squarely at the door of those who promoted such disastrous teaching, and I assert as strongly as possible that it is *distressing*, it is *damaging*, and it is *dangerous* in the extreme.

At the end of 1986 John Wimber ran one of his healing conferences in the Harrogate conference centre. I had one of the delegates staying at my home and while I did not feel that it would be courteous to enter into controversy with a guest, she insisted on raising this subject for discussion, so we talked about it together.

As I outlined the arguments and the data set out in these paragraphs, my guest replied, 'I do not want to throw out the baby with the bathwater.' There can only be one response to this sentiment: it is not a *baby* in that bathwater, it is a *tiger*, and we need to recognise that.

This miracle-healing teaching so often increases the agony of those who suffer. How cruel to say that people are not healed because they do not have sufficient faith! Here is someone who is *suffering*, who responds to an appeal for healing, and who is not healed. Such a person now has *two* problems with which to cope: a sense of severe spiritual inadequacy, *and* the original illness. I feel strongly about it as a doctor, and I feel even more strongly about it as a Christian, because this kind of teaching steals from believers the comfort of Scripture.

In *2 Corinthians 1.3-4* we are told — *Blessed be God, even the Father of our Lord Jesus Christ, the Father of mercies, and the God of all comfort; who comforteth us in all our tribulation, that we may be able to comfort them which are in any trouble, by the comfort wherewith we ourselves are comforted of God*. There are times when sickness and affliction come upon us so that we might be equipped to minister comfort to others who will tread a similar path.

Not long ago one of the workers in the beach mission which I serve in was travelling on his bicycle when he was run down by a lorry and rendered paraplegic. He has no natural parents, but many of us have sat by his bedside in an endeavour to help him. We have tried our best, but do you know from where he has received the greatest comfort? We wrote to Joni Eareckson to tell her about his situation and she responded with a wonderful letter, warm, caring, concerned. That letter from a quadraplegic woman, who has written of her terrible accident and the struggles through which she went before she found a resting place in Christ, did immeasurably more for our young man than any comfort we could minister. Why? Because she had lain where he lay; she had been through it. She knew exactly the torture of his spirit and the turmoil of his mind, and so she was able to comfort him with the comfort wherewith God had comforted her.

Surely we can look at the lessons of history and see that this has always been so. The Christian church has been a suffering church. God has had great purposes in affliction. We think of Fanny Crosby the hymnwriter, blind from the age of six weeks. We think of William Cowper, another great hymnwriter, with his fits of depression. We think of Amy Carmichael, so often secluded in her home because of illness. I think of Dr Mary Verguese who was also a paraplegic, and yet God so used her that she was able to write, 'He took away my legs and He gave me wings.' There have been many down the years who have found that this is so.

We have a great responsibility in our fellowships to foster a warm, caring, praying community so that those who are sick, whether it be in mind or body, will know that there is a company of people who really *care*, and who really pray. We need to have a great concern for those who are afflicted, for they are part of the body of Christ, and if they hurt, we must feel the hurt along with them. But we should never forget that the greatest comfort is often ministered by those who have trodden the same path of suffering.

A final thought, yet one of prime importance, is that this present wave of miraculous healing teaching diminishes our Christian testimony. My sister-in-law was in her thirties when she developed cancer of the oesophagus. Initially her condition was misdiagnosed, understandably because of the difficulty of the situation, and by the time the correct diagnosis was made the condition was inoperable. Before she died she gathered the family together, and around the piano they sang:

> *I am not skilled to understand*
> *What God has willed, what God has planned.*
> *I only know at God's right hand*
> *Stands One Who is my Saviour.*

Here, surely, is the *real* testimony of a Christian — not that I am healed in my body, but that I can look death in the face and know that because of the merits of a redeeming Saviour, I am going to be able to face God with equanimity, knowing that at God's right hand there stands a Saviour Who is mine. Surely there is nothing more important than that, and anything which detracts from that overwhelming truth does despite to the Gospel of the grace of God. I submit that in these days Christian people are getting things out of perspective and are losing their appreciation of the heart of the Gospel — at God's right hand stands One Who is my Saviour.

The great dangers, then, of this miraculous healing teaching are, first, that it discredits the person of Christ because of the very obvious failures, when we claim to serve a Saviour Who never fails. Secondly, it undermines the Word, because it elevates a new form of 'revelation' — so-called words of knowledge or prophecy. Thirdly, it deceives Christians and breeds a race of gullible believers, taken in by virtually anything. Fourthly, it increases the agony of suffering, being so often distressing, and even disastrous. Fifthly, it removes Christian comfort. And finally, it all too often diminishes Christian testimony.

Further reading:

The Charismatic Phenomenon
Peter Masters & John C. Whitcomb

'The Charismatic Phenomenon' provides biblical answers to the questions raised today concerning the nature and authenticity of present-day 'gifts' compared with the signs and wonders of the early church.

Questions dealt with in short, direct chapters include the following:— Are they the same gifts? What was the purpose of the gifts in New Testament times? Should we personally seek the gifts? What about the signs of Mark 16? Does God heal today? Why don't the gifts stay until Christ comes? Shouldn't we exorcise demons today?

First issued in 1982, 'The Charismatic Phenomenon' has gone through six reprints and has been translated into several languages. This latest edition has been revised and extended. 113 pages, paperback.